A look at
in Bradfield ‎
and the Surrounding area

(From the High Middle Ages)

CW00504777

*I wish this account of Bradfield Dale and the
surrounding area to be In Memoriam for Barbara
Mary, my late wife, who always found so enjoyable
an unhurried tour of the beautiful countryside of
that region. For over forty years Barbara helped me
with the collecting and the write-up of local history
and I am much indebted to her for such kindness
and generous support.*

Joe Castle

© Joe Castle 2008
All rights reserved. No part of this publication
may be reproduced, stored in a retrieval system,
or transmitted in any form or by any means
without the prior permission of the copyright holder.

(Reprinted 2009)

ISBN 0-901100-81-1

Designed and Printed by Northend Creative Print Solutions,
Sheffield S8 0TZ
Tel: 0114 250 0331 Fax: 0114 250 0676
Email: ks@northend.co.uk

PREFACE

To mark the occasion of having, in August 1998, completed fifty years of collecting the local history of the Wadsley, Wisewood and Worrall areas, I penned a lengthy manuscript titled 'Roads to Worrall' and this I gave to the Marlcliffe Primary School (where, for the first few years of my educational life I was a pupil) for the purpose of producing a booklet to sell and raise funds for the school and this they did.

Eight years later and desirous, again, of putting pen to paper I selected for this project, and beyond my usual boundary, the lovely countryside areas of Bradfield Dale. My discoveries are revealed in the following pages but when reading them I ask you to remember that research of events 500 years ago cannot guarantee accuracy.

Exceedingly good fortune was to come my way through my 'delvings' and yielding some splendid bonus stories which, in part, I will share with you. First, there was the priest/amateur gardener, a part of whose ancestry was traced back to Wigtwizzle, who was mainly responsible for the creation of the gardens at Frogmore for Queen Charlotte. Some background material about this reverend gentleman was unknown at Windsor and so that part of the handwritten manuscript was retained for use in the Royal Archives there. That, indeed, I considered a privilege!

Another discovery was of the little known hamlet, near Ugghill, of Romesker (with its very unusual wayside Cross) and from which place a native, having the same name as the group of farms, married a member of the Hollis family of Rotherham who were cutlers. A descendant set up as a Merchant in London and after becoming very wealthy he and his sons and grandsons were among the principal benefactors of the oldest educational institution in the United States of America, namely the Harvard University.

The U.S.A. featured, too, in the third 'lucky' find when, after a very long but most fascinating journey, I travelled from Wigtwizzle to Washington and no less a home than that of the President, but it was Vice-President Richard Cheney who was the subject of this trace though and this he not only found interesting but also a prompt to look at his Family Tree. Let's hope we 'got it right'.

Time, they say, flies and so, dear reader, DEO GRATIAS, I have now completed sixty years of pursuing what I consider to be a useful and absorbing hobby. Opportunity once more to 'celebrate', I reckoned, and so what better I thought than to prepare a slimmed-down version of the original, 100 page and hand written manuscript so that all who wished to do so could enjoy this perambulation in the comfort of a fireside chair. This modest volume is the result.

Lastly, I have the greatest pleasure in saying that, over such a very long time, many, many people have given generously of their time, labours and knowledge to assist in my endeavours and as many of them as I can remember by name I do so at the conclusion of this slim booklet.

HALLEFELDE IN THORNSETT
A 1270 grant
probably dating from the Furnival Charter

"KNOW ALL MEN present and to come that I, Thomas Ffurnival the son of Lord Thomas Ffurnival have Given, Granted and, by this my present writing have confirmed to Ellys of Ugghill, and all men of Ugghill, Nether Bradfield, Thornseat and Hawksworth the herbiage as it lies in length and breadth between Ugghillbrook, Eventrevick and the way leading from Hope to Sheffield, Bradrake, Seven Stones in Horderon, Weanstone to the waters of Agden for the depasturing and agisting of their own propper cattle to be taken yearly without hindrance of me or of my heirs as they have held the same to farm at Will of my ancestors... rendering to me and my heirs four Marks in Silver at two terms of the year, viz. one half at the ffeast of Penticost and the other half at the ffeast of St. Martin..."

THE 1297 CHARTER

The Third Lord Furnival gave 'to the Yeomen, Freeholders of Stannington, Morewood, Hallom and Fulwood herbiage and foliage throughout the Forest of Rivelin in length and breadth between Malen Bridge, Belhag and Whitely Wood on the one part and a place called Stanage and the Common Way which leads from Derwent to Sheffield on the other...'

In the 1950/51 year edition of the Sheffield Clarion Ramblers Handbook, pp128-150 can be found details of this vast area. Of most interest to our exercise are Thornseat in Bradfield Dale and Hawksworth, being in that part of Bradfield which ends at Howden Edge. The Seven Stones circle was beside the Sheffield, Bradfield, Moscar Cross and Hope ancient Bridleway and some 600 yards, S.S.E., of the Cutthroat Bridge.

HALLEFELDE – early mentions of

In volume No. 11 of the Bradfield Local History Group's 1988 publication, and under the heading of 'Hallfield' one reads that, while doing some research upon her ancestors Miss Beryl Greaves came across much material about the property and this "she kindly passed on to us and for which we are extremely grateful."

The earliest reference to Hallfield in Bradfield is in 1318 when 'Adam Heggar fil William Heggar de Romesker dedi de Adam, fil William Hawksworth and Beatrice his wife a piece of land called Hallefelde in Thornsett'. This, I interpret to mean that William Heggar de Romesker's son, Adam surrended/conveyed to Adam, son of William and Beatrice Hawksworth such a parcel of land.

ROMESKER: the name and locality

The name occurs in most useful details compiled by antiquarian, John Wilson of Broomhead Hall, upon the subject of Crosses and Milestones of ancient origin and which at one time were to be found in the enormous Parish of Bradfield.

4

Mr Wilson refers to the 'Bridding Wife Cross in Romesker' and this, veteran rambler and compiler of the Clarion Ramblers Handbook, Mr G.H.B. Ward believed... 'This clearly points to a Medieval Cross to which the Anciente went to pray, to Vow and to wish, etc. This is a most interesting name but the site is now not known'.

While researching his book 'Pre-Register Genealogy and Lost Place Names' a Mr C.A. Ramskir came across an "OLD Deed of 1385 relating to the Close under Bridding Wife Cross in Romesker and called 'Crimbles' passing from Robert Romesker to R. Hayteth. Many Medieval Crosses existed at one time in the Bradfield area and some of these are listed on p124 of the Clarion Ramblers Handbook for the years 1932/33. Some were Catholic wayside crosses where a prayer could be offered while others were simply incised stones bearing route directions and called guide stones. But, exactly what was the purpose of that at Romesker? Numerous variants are provided in the Oxford English Dictionary and also in Henry Sweet's 1897 published Dictionary of Anglo Saxon Words and these include: Bryd (wife), Brydian (married woman), Bridlian (bride), Brude (bride), Briddan (to pray, worship). From these one deduces that in, or at the borders of what would have been the tiniest of hamlets, stood a Celtic-type cross where lawfully married women went either to pray, for a gossip or perhaps barter goods, food. On the other hand another interpretation can be placed upon the word 'bride'. It can be a shortened form of bridle and this, of course, is a part of a horse's headgear, and one recalls that in those times the principal form of transportation was by such animals.

Of the other words used a close is a piece of land or a field while, again, in the aforementioned dictionaries are to be found variants of the word 'Crimble'. One of these means to corrugate or wrinkle a smooth surface. Pondering these possibilities one wonders if the explanation is that at Romesker in Ugghillwoodside stood a cross which was intended for directional purposes and positioned near to a ploughed field?

Actually, I have found an earlier reference to Romesker than that of 1318 and this is revealed by Mr Ramskir who discovered that William de Romesker is believed to have been born in 1250 and it was his son Adam who, in 1295, received from William Whytlee a Grant of Land at Bradfield and being at Hallefelde in Thornsett this being a gift from Thomas, son of Thomas, Lord Furnival. The relevant document being signed and sealed at Bradfield. Presumably, this would be the piece of land which Adam surrendered in 1318.

(For guidance the name Heggar means a hedgeman or hedger, a dweller in an enclosure).

At the Sheffield Court in 1399 Thomas de Lockesley surrendered a messuage and two crofts at Ugghillwoodside and also an acre called Ryacre to the use of Thomas de Romesker.

THE FORESTER OF HALLFIELD

On December 22nd 1440, at Sheffield Court, the Forester of Hallfield said that

5

two young trees had been destroyed by a William Drake and for this he was duly fined four pence.

The very existence of a Forester employed by the Lord of the Manor at Hallfield suggests that this employee must also have been responsible for the maintenance of Rivelin Forest and the plentiful supply of game and of boar found therein, the vast area being used by the Lord and his friends for hunting purposes. One wonders if the Forester actually did live at a messuage on the site where the house was built?

Referring back to the 1440 Sheffield Court, it was declared there that Thomas de Shawe, of Hallom had purposely driven twenty three swine from Pannage of Hallfield 'to the damage of the Lord' but despite his denial he was fined no less than ten shillings. Pannage was pasturage for pigs. It was at this sitting of the Court that the name of the Forester of Hallfield was revealed and it was Roger Tyler. He must have been a busy man of late for his reportings back to the Lord of the Manor resulted in fines of two pence each for fishing without consent 'in the waters of the Don' for Henry Golding, John Smyth, Will de-Wode, John Trippet, Richard Shemeld, John de-Stanyforf, Robert Attwell, Richard Attwell and William Drake. Thomas de-Birley was in trouble for 'taking away dry wood' without consent.

LAND IN ROMESKER

Twelve months later, at the Sheffield Court appeared Richard Roger, his wife Joan and their two sons, William and John where they 'took of the Lord' two crofts called Mitecrofts in Romesker, to be held for a term of twenty-five years. Among the jurors at that Court was Thomas Romesker. Long, long afterwards the ruined remains of a property by name Mitehouse remained adjacent to a close called The Croft and from there a track led to Roger House on the other side of Blindside Lane. The Thomas Romesker referred to died in 1445. Three months later, in the 19th year of the reign of Henry VI it was 'found' that (by the Jurors of the soke of Bradfield – John Morewood of The Oakes, Robert Mokeson, Thomas de Shawe (cooper), William de Morton, John Bromehead of Bradfield, John Marriott, Thomas Smallbend, John de Wirrall, Thomas Romesker, William Hudson, John Thompson, John Tag, John Bacon and John de Greve (the elder) 'William, son of William de Hawksworth the elder had wrongfully occupied a messuage, an oxgang, 11 acres of assorted land (with appertunances) in Hawksworth which Thomas Hawksworth, the younger brother of the said William had from the gift and surrender of his aforesaid father, Thomas Hawksworth. He was fined six pence. It is interesting to note that 1456 saw the marriage of Maud Wortley and one Walter de Hawksworth and thus, one presumes linking the two families unless this had already been done by a previous marriage.

ENTER THE WENTWORTHS

In her notes about Hallfield, Miss Greaves states that in... "1708 Hallfield was sold to Thomas Wentworth, of Wentworth Woodhouse," but more about that later.

I first came across the name Wentyworth in relation to the area in the reign of King Henry VI when, in 1442 a quit-claim declared that… "Cecily, Widow of William de Wentyworth… to John de Romesker, his heirs and assigns… all that (her) right to one messuage and six and a half acres of land hustler in Bradfield."

The earliest record I have traced of the Greaves family living in the Dungworth area is that of an appearance at Sheffield Court, on October 9th 1469 when John Greave made an application to the Lord of the Manor for leave to hold – after the decease of his father, John, and whose heir he was – one tenement and certain lands at Dungworth and this was granted to "him, his heirs and assigns" and he to pay the Lord each year the sum of six shillings and three pence. He did fealty (pay homage) to the Lord, paid him 11s 3d on account and was subsequently admitted as a tenant. In turn, his son John, on September 30th 1501 made application to continue holding the same property and renting the land and this was approved.

ROMESKER AFFAIRS

William Romesker said born c1500 made a Will which made six of his seven children wondering if and when they were to inherit anything at all simply because their father had stipulated that this depended upon whether his eldest son, John, did in the seven years following his father's demise, either marry or live peacefully. He took the first course and thereby denied his brothers and sisters anything. A vital key as to the exact location of where the Romeskers lived is provided by the mention of their home croft being at Edgefield. Our aforementioned John at the time of his marriage, on May 16th 1559, held a messuage and two closes at a place called the Ryacre (probably that held by his ancestor, Thomas Romesker in 1399). The meaning of Ryacre is suggestive of a place for the growing of Rye fodder. I wonder if it was John's brother Robert Romesker who, at Bradfield on November 29th 1573, married a member of the locally-based Greaves family, in the person of one Ellen. Another link between the two families was created some 13 years later when John, possibly the son of John Romesker, married Isobel Greaves. Henry, probably a son of the 1559-wed John Romesker, and who was born December 1563, is recorded as having, in 1613 in the vicinity of Hannett House several 'parcels of land on both sides of the waters of the Steyne, also pighilles and crofts'. It is believed that early in the 1600s the Romesker family moved from Bradfield to Sheffield (a fact we will deal with later) and the very last two Romesker entries appearing in the Registers of Bradfield Chapel were those of the burials of Robert, in 1598 and Ellen, his wife, three years later, they having been married twenty-five years.

As regards Hannett House (about which more notes later) it is known that the owner in 1617 was one John Beighton and that he had let the place to James Bagshawe.

7

Hallfield House

GREAVES FAMILY OF UGGHILLWOODSIDE

At a session of the Sheffield Court held on October 3rd 1565, John Greaves, said then to be of Ugghillwoodside, gave-surrended a messuage and one oxgang of land thereabouts for the use of his wife, Helen and their children, Raph, Robert, James and John. Fifty years later a descendant of the same place, in turn gave the like house and land to his son Raph upon this young man's marriage to Ellen, a daughter of Richard Bromehead of Thornsett for their use during the remaining lifetime of John Greaves and thereafter it was to become theirs to own. It seems almost certain that the Romesker and the Greaves families were neighbours at Ugghillswoodside.

THE GREAVES OF HALLFIELD

Bearing in mind that there also were branches of the Greaves family at the Yew Trees, Hopwood House, Holdsworth, Ewden, Morewood, Thornsett and Spinkhouse and that the successive generations were given like Christian names, nothing can be certain before the commencement of Parish Registers in 1559. Therefore, despite intensive and time consuming research I cannot say assuredly, who were the earliest members of the Greaves family residing at what originally would have been a small farm at Hallfield. Miss Greaves – a descendant – believes that in 1565 Raph Greaves was there together with Ellen his wife and children who were called... Diones, Isobel, Ellen, Agnes, John and Thomas.

A contradiction, however, to this is shown in the two Pedigrees of the Greaves family which Joseph Hunter compiled and appear in his Familae Minorum Gentium and there one reads that while Ellen was the mother of both John and Thomas their father was one Robert and not Raph!

SOMETHING ABOUT JOHN GREAVES

It is believed that John was actually born at Shephouse and duly baptised at Penistone Church in 1634. Of his childhood and youth I have, unfortunately, discovered not a thing. His father was Nicholas and, in 1652, probably with an eye to eventually having much to gain from such a 'Union' he arranged for John to be married to Gertrude, one of the daughters of Henry Bright, of Whirlow, a gentleman. Her marriage portion was £500 and John was given both Hallfield and several other estate properties. The couple were married on April 19th 1652 and it is a presumption that they straightaway moved in the Hallfield house and where they both lived together for many years; John dying on June 4th 1692.

Nicholas could be said to have made a very shrewd move by this 'arrangement' since the Brights of Whirlow, Brincliffe, Fulwood and of Dore were, indeed, a very wealthy family owning vast amounts of land and properties both in and around the Sheffield area. In his 1999 published work 'We Of Our Bounty' Dr George Tolley provides much biographical detail of many who were chosen to be Sheffield Church Burgesses and as to be expected, a number were members of the Bright family. Henry, Gertrude's father was one such serving for twenty-one years between 1652 and 1673. Born in 1600 he was baptised at Sheffield Parish Church on the 1st of January 1601. It is likely that when Henry married Isobel Romesker he took to be his bride none other than the daughter of that John Romesker who, in 1586, had married Isobel Greaves, then of Ugghillwoodside. At the time of the marriage Henry was residing at Whirlow. Henry's father was John Bright, also of the same place and his wife was Grace, a daughter of Anthony Bright, of Dore. Anthony's brother, Robert had no less than four wives, the last being Isobel, the widow of John Romesker. Isobel's mother, of course, was a member of the Greaves family. One of Robert Bright's sisters, namely Elizabeth, became the wife of Nicholas Birley, of 'The Yews' at Worrall and it was one of their descendants, Mary Birley who became the wife of Joseph, a grandson of John Marriott of Ugghill, and whose own wife, Ellen, was one of the children of Raph Greaves of Hallfield.

THE CHILDREN OF JOHN AND GERTUDE GREAVES

Bapt. 1653 4th March at Bradfield...
> Gertrude who died on February 23rd 1672.

Bapt. 1655 27th January at Bradfield...
> Elizabeth, co-heir who, at Bradfield on 13th July 1675 married Samuel Morewood of The Oakes, Bradfield, he then being aged 27. Their marriage lasted some forty years until Samuel died in 1715. Elizabeth's demise came in 1727. The Morewood ancestory can be traced back to 1444 when William Morewood was involved in certain land transactions.

Bapt. 1657 ? March at Bradfield...
> Anne, who died and was Bradfield buried 1st July 1658.

Bapt. 1659 8th March at Bradfield...
> John, who died and was Bradfield buried 7th September 1667.

Bapt. 1663 14th June at Bradfield...
> Thomas who was said to have died before his father (1692) and, with him joined in the cutting off of the entail and thereby restricting the descent of the estate to a designated line of heirs.

Bapt. 1673 1st March at Bradfield...
> Mary, who at the time of her father John's death in 1692, was only nineteen years of age and therefore subject to Guardianship. More details about her later.

Bapt. 1675 9th December at Bradfield...
> Henry who died in 1686 being Bradfield buried on September 7th.

Believed in 1656 at Bradfield...
> Ellen who was to marry a John Greaves of Bakewell, Derbyshire.

THOMAS, THE BROTHER OF JOHN GREAVES

It was from Mr Hunter's Pedigree of the Greaves family, Ms 329 and p801 that the following information was obtained, namely that Thomas was the second son of Nicholas and Elizabeth Greaves and that he married a sister of John

Wainwright, of Midhope. The couple had one son, John, who was to live at Shephouse and he married one of the daughters of Robert Blackburn of Alderman's Head. Their son, John, was much embittered by the entailment of the Hallfield estate by his relatives believing that he had some rightful claim to the property and land but this did not come about. In fact, Hallfield occupier and his uncle, John Greaves, died in 1692 intestate and so the estate passed to his three daughters, Ellen, Elizabeth and Mary, as all their brothers had died. John and his brother, Thomas – also of Shephouse – were the cousins of John Wainwright, of Gill Royd Farm, Deepcar whose principal interest was the rearing of sheep and these, numbering 360, were watched over by son Timothy who was their shepherd.

THE LAST WILL AND TESTAMENT OF NICHOLAS GREAVES

This was dated 12th of February, 1662 and by it he bequeathed to 'John Greaves, sonne of Thomas Greaves one hundred pounds when he becomes one and twenty'. John, the son of John Greaves received 'six lambes'. Other bequests were made to the members of his family and also to his servants. John Greaves of Hallfield, was the executor of the Will and he, after seeing all expenses had been paid and the bequests carried out, received the 'rest of my goods, cattell and chattels'. He allowed his nephew, John, to continue residing at Shephouse.

GUARDIANSHIP OF MARY GREAVES

It has to be a presumption that, following the death of Gertrude, the wife of John Greaves on September 2nd 1687, the widower was left at Hallfield with his daughter, Mary, then only 14 years of age and probably some servants as both his other daughters, Ellen and Elizabeth, had married and were living elsewhere. Five years later, Mary then 19, found herself the only Greaves in Hallfield when her father died. Under 21 she was obliged to seek Guardianship for the next two years and the choice fell upon John Woodhead of a neighbouring farm called Woodseats. But, why this selection? A little pondering of the following facts could provide a solution.

On August 29th 1589 at Bradfield Chapel, Ellen, a daughter of Raph Greaves married John, (a son of John Marriott) of Ugghill. His brother was Thomas Marriott of both Wath and of Kinder, Derbyshire. Thomas, a grandson of Thomas was to become known as 'Thomas the Younger' and this gentleman took to be his bride Mary, the 15 year old daughter of Robert Woodhead, of Woodseats Farm. Robert's father was John Woodhead who in 1714 had married Mary Croyden and in addition to Robert the couple had two other children, being Thomas, who died in infancy and Dorothy (baptised in 1722) who became the wife of Benjamin, a son of Nicholas Stead of Onesacre. Robert Woodhead's uncle, George Woodhead of Wigtwizzle was later to move to Hallfield. His son and heir, John of Nether Bradfield, also married a member of the Stead family in the person of Elizabeth, one of the children of Thomas Stead and also of Onesacre.

THE 9th JUNE 1692 INVENTORY OF JOHN GREAVES OF HALLFIELD

I once had an actual reproduction copy of the 'True and Perfect Inventory of and Singular, His goods, chattels and cattels of John Greaves of Hallfield in the Chapelry of Bradfield and County of York, late deceased .. Appraized the ninth day of June Anno Domini 1692 by us whose names are subscribed..' (and being Jonathan Shaw, Nicholas Stead, Thomas Revel and John Greaves) but it has been misplaced. However, I did make a copy and, with some useful notes, it reads as follows:

	£	s	d
Imprimis... His purse and apparell	20	00	0
In the House... one long table one buffet forme and three			
little buffets		15	0
three chaires		05	0
one table		04	0
one longe chaire		01	6
In the Dyning Room... one table with back seatted one			
form and one little table	01	15	0
one long settle		15	0
three ceiled chaires		15	0
three little chaires and two buffets		05	0
eleven quishions and two carpits	00	19	0
one bed and bedding in the little Parlour	03	00	0
one cupboard	01	00	0
two chests	00	16	0
three chaires and three buffets	00	13	0
a sideboard cloath and one window curtain	00	02	0
In the Buttry... one safe and one drinke cupboard	01	00	0
one table and buffets (nine)	01	00	6
one box forme	01	00	6
two little boxes and three shelves	00	02	0
one buffet and one deske	00	03	6
In the Old Man's Chamber... one bed with furniture	02	00	0
two other beds and furniture	05	00	0
one trunkel bed	00	05	0
one hanging presse	01	00	0
one cupboard with bedding and eight qushions	01	14	0
one deske one close stool and one buffett	00	05	6
one range one fyre shawel and one paire tongs	00	03	6
In the Best Chamber... one bed with furniture	05	00	0
one square table	00	13	0
two chests with certaine wooden wares	01	04	0
five chaires and six buffets	01	06	0
one box with frame and coverings	00	08	0
In the Closet... one chest and some bees wax	00	10	0

one silver cup with tumbler and one silver spoone	04	00	0
one little table and eighteen spoones	00	06	6
eight dossen of trenchers and wooden wares	00	15	0
one chaire	00	01	0
In the Nicholas Chamber... one halfe-headed bed	01	00	0
In the Schoole Master Chamber... one bed with furniture, chaire	02	03	6
In the Margaret Chamber... one bed and three chaires	01	15	0
In the Great Chamber... one halfe-headed bed one great			
arke one chaire and two beds	03	05	0
one chaire seavon boards certaine spokes			
wooden vessels	00	16	0
In the Parlour... one clocke	01	05	0
In the Chamber over the House... four arkes	01	11	0
one arke with certaine salt meat in it	04	11	0
one arke with some meat in it	04	00	0
one trunkel bed with furniture	00	10	0
one load of salt	00	06	0
In the Wash House... one salting vat and four barrells	01	16	0
four barrells more	00	14	0
In the Milk House... two loomes and two kits	00	07	0
six oxen	26	00	0
five kine and a bull	16	10	0
one other cow and three heiffers	10	00	0
three horses	11	10	0
one little calfe	00	10	0
one hundred twenty six weathers	34	13	0
eighty three cupples	20	15	0
one hundred twenty eight geld ewes and hoggs	24	00	0
In the Wain House... two waines and certaine husbandry gaires	12	00	0
In the Barnes... one shemeld waine three arkes and a fann	06	05	0
seed and plowage	05	00	0
yoaks teams buckets buckles and horse gaires	01	02	0
three saddles and other husbandry gaires	01	12	0
potts pans and other brasse wares	05	10	0
pewter	03	14	0
coverlets and blankets	02	06	0
certaine lynninges	05	09	0
two ranges tong fyre shovels and other			
hustlements (in and about the house)	<u>02</u>	<u>00</u>	<u>0</u>

	Total	272	06	0
Debts Inwards		45	05	0
Debts Outwards		<u>235</u>	<u>01</u>	<u>0</u>

Apprized by us; Jonathan Shaw, Nicholas Stead, Thomas Revell, John Greaves.

Some observations

As regards the Schoole Master's Chamber, this gives reason to reflect upon the education of those times. Yeomen had little time for teaching their employees, since that might bring about 'opposition' to conditions, tasks. There were a few exceptions, however, to this line of thought and encouragement, for example, was shown in the Parish of Penistone by the Greaves family who allowed the rents obtained from some of their land to be used for the tuition of a few children in the South Aisle of the Parish Church. Later, Penistone Old Grammar School received such rent from land the Greaves family owned at Hunshelf, per Thomas Greaves and John Greaves, amounting to 3s 4d a year. Relative, Ralph Greaves also paid the school 3s 0d for use of some land at 'Storthe', in the area. At that time one of the Trustees of the Penistone Grammar School was a John Greaves of Hallfield and so, when one reads of the existence of a Schoole Master's Room or Chamber at that property it really does make sense with probably successive heads of families employing a resident tutor for their children. Certainly, so far as I can discover, there was no schooling of groups of children in the Bradfield, Stannington, Dungworth, Worrall, Ugghill or Loxley areas at the beginning of the 1600s and what precious little knowledge the vast majority of the poorer people had to pass on to their children was that which they had received from their parents, usually verbally since few in those times would be able to write.

But tuition there must have been at the homes and the farms of the wealthy in the Bradfield Chapelry but by whom, exactly where and for what periods is hard to establish. Indeed, there are very few references to schoolmasters; in fact in the Bradfield Chapelry Registers for the whole of the time between 1560 and 1720 there are only two statements among the many hundreds of burials and baptisms that a person held that profession. The first mention was made when, John, a son of William Dawson was baptised on January 12th 1612, his father being a 'Scholem' while twenty-two years later, on July 16th 1634 there was buried one 'Mr Cottrell' described as a 'Scoulmayster'.

RICHARD SPOONE'S BEQUEST

It was after the enactment of a bequest in the Last Will and Testament of the Stannington landowner and yeoman, Richard Spoone, and of date May 23rd 1652 that a limited amount of education in that and the adjoining areas commenced. He left a property by the name of Symhouse and with it a 'close thereunto with a kilne...' to the four Feoffes for them at discretion to sell, to let or to dispose of at a valuable rent and to... "bestow the revenues, issues, profits... for and towards the paying for the learning of poor children within the said Byerlow whose parents are willing but not able to keep them to the school." Two points here to question. Firstly does 'to the school' actually infer that one already existed despite the belief that Mr Spoone's bequest was the means of providing one? And, secondly, since – as he recognised – most parents needed every child who was capable of helping on the land, etc., to augment

14

the meagre family income, anyway, would there have been a big demand for a school?

Presumably, tuition for the handful of scholars who were privileged to take up the generous offer was in a room at the home of the schoolmaster and the exact location of this is believed to have been at Underbank near Stannington. Records exist which show that two years after the bequest, one Richard Creswick, a layman, was the schoolmaster. Was he, I ponder, that Richard Creswick who, at Bradfield on December 4th 1628, married Ann Morton or was the 'scolem' in fact their son, Richard who was baptised on February 28th 1630? One imagines that it would have been the latter and that he not only taught the children at Stannington but also at Wigtwizzle since it was in that locality near the Old Booth Farm a schoolmaster by the same name collapsed and later died in 1693. Private tuition is also mentioned in the Last Will and Testament of Edmund Waterhouse, the Younger, of Swinnock Hall in the Chapelry. Dated 3rd July 1687, the testator declared that his... "mind and will is that my beloved brothers, Nicholas Stead and Henry Waterhouse have the tuition of my said daughter (Elizabeth) and to whose care I commit her..."

THE LOW BRADFIELD SCHOOL

Now, into our 'picture' steps Thomas Marriott (The Elder). He was born on 23rd July 1643, baptised son of John Marriott of Ugghill who, on March 5th 1633 had married Ann Revill. Thomas had a sister, Anne, who married a 'clerk' by the name of John Hoole at Sheffield Parish Church on November 15th 1659 and this cleric had two spells serving as a Minister at Bradfield Chapel, from the first being ejected because of his non-conformity. Much more information about Mr Hoole I have included in my manuscript 'Families associated with the early days of Underbank Chapel' which is lodged with the Local Studies Department of Sheffield City Library.

In times gone by it was customary for the first-born son to inherit a family estate and so when John Marriott died this should have automatically passed to John, a brother of Thomas, but for reasons unknown he was bypassed and the recipient was John's son, Thomas. This young man however, died at the age of 25, very shortly after marrying and left the estate to his uncle, Thomas Marriott (the Elder) who married a lady by the name of Martha Lee. There were no children from the marriage and his wife pre-deceased Thomas by her death in 1704. The couple are said to have lived in Sheffield town, where Thomas had many 'an iron in the fire' being not only a Warden at the Parish Church but also over the years one of the Governors of Sheffield Grammar School, a Town Trustee, Town Collector in 1669 and for twenty-four years he was a Church Burgess. Described as a Merchant, Thomas had interests in lead mining in Derbyshire. Thomas and his brother John had another brother called Joseph and it was his son, Thomas, who was to become known as Thomas Marriott (the Younger) and it was he, as already mentioned, who married a 15 year old girl in the person of Mary Woodhead.

Two years after his wife's demise, Thomas Marriott (the Elder) 'surrended a copyhold house, croft and garden in Nether Bradfield to the use of the Reverend William Bagshawe, then Minister of the Stannington Chapel and ten others appointed as Trustees for a school and for the habitation of the schoolmaster', and by a Deed dated March 10th 1706, he granted 'to the Trustees for the maintaining of the schoolmaster, and as a recompense for his instructing 20 poor children in Dungworth and Bradfield Byerlows in the Chapelry of Bradfield whose parents should be willing but not able to pay for the learning, a yearly rent charge of £10'. (This information is taken from the Charity Comm. Report for 1828 – Ecclesfield, Low Bradfield School and see p11).

The income of the said school was boosted nine years later when, following his death, Thomas Marriott (the Elder) bequeathed 'The Houfsing and two crofts which I bought of George Hall I give to the School at Stannington for the teaching of seavon or eight children to be chofen out of Stanningmoorwood and Storrs by the Trustees of the school'. The original school premises were replaced by a new building in 1854 and education at Underbank ceased in 1911. The Stannington Church of England School opened in 1830 initially as a place of learning for all who desired to be educated, and some fourteen years later it became a day school.

SCHOOLING AT ONESACRE

Another educational venture in the Chapelry of Bradfield for youngsters was made possible by a bequest contained in the Last Will and Testament of wealthy bachelor, land and property owner, Thomas Stead of Onesacre Hall, near Oughtibridge although judging by the placing of it in the document one wonders if it was an after-thought or the result of a suggestion. Appearing right at the very end of the Will, his Executor was instructed to invest the sum of £50 and the interest therefrom to be used for the payment... 'of the Master for the time being of the school at Onesacre... for the purpose of instructing four such poor children in reading and writing'. This, again, suggests that some form of education was already being taught in the hamlet and perhaps in one of the cottages near to the hall. The children eligible for selection lived in a wide catchment area including Worrall, Oughtibridge and naturally, Onesacre itself. They were hand-picked by Thomas Stead, Executor and nephew of the Testator who further decreed that his nephew and his heirs had the 'right of appointing such master for the time being for ever'. Dated 3rd of November 1763 and witnessed by J.O. Bonsor, John Milns and George Crawshaw. From such humble a beginning the 'cottage room' school was to flourish and 34 years later, with the generous help of Miss Sarah Greaves, of Worrall Hall, there came into being the 'Onesacre School Foundation'. By that time the number of pupils enjoying free tuition had increased to a dozen and financially it would seem the 'Onesacre Endowed School' enjoyed a good basic income. In my booklet 'Roads to Worrall' I have provided more detail about happenings there. Children continued to walk in all weathers to and from the little one room seat of learning until there opened on March 20th 1886 the new school at Wharncliffe Side. Onesacre then closed but the whitewashed cottage where it was held is still very plain to see on the bankside.

THE UPPER BRADFIELD SCHOOL

The opening of a school to educate some sixty boys and girls at Upper Bradfield is said to have been made possible principally through the generosity of Mrs Sarah Rimington (who we have already 'met') of Broomhead Hall. To enable it to be built she first purchased a cottage with its adjoining piece of land. The school first accepted children in 1841. Perhaps one shouldn't put 'two and two together' but I'm going to here simply because I firmly believe that the good lady was 'nudged' into the project by a Curate at that time of Bradfield, namely the Reverend William Gill who was ordained as a Deacon at the Chapel in 1829. But his meagre stipend was greatly enhanced when he was invited by the Rimingtons to live-in at Broomhead Hall and tutor their ever increasing number of children. So between those and his parochial duties he was kept busy. Sarah's husband James was only son and heir of John Rimington of Hillsborough Hall and it was he who was responsible for a great deal of the administrative work involved in the planning and the opening of the Sheffield, Wadsley and Langsett Turnpike Road in 1805. Who was his great, great grandfather? Why, none other than the guardian of Mary Greaves, namely John Woodhead of Woodseats Farm.

Sarah Rimington's father was Samuel Broomhead of the Mount, Sheffield and following her marriage to James on September 1st 1817 the couple had nine children, the first being Sarah Caroline who was baptised at Bradfield on September 30th 1819 while William was the youngest being christened also at Bradfield on August 26th 1834.

The Reverend William Gill married Mary Anne Heywood, and eventually they took up residence at 'The Yews', Worrall where they began their own family. Additional to his tutoring at Broomhead Hall and Curacy duties at Bradfield, Mr Gill was required to also be Curate of Stannington Church but this served him well as in 1846, resigning the Bradfield post and terminating his employ with the Rimingtons, he was appointed as Vicar of Stannington. Bradfield Upper School finally closed in July 1932.

THE USE OF CHAMBERS

Reference was made in the Inventory of the 'Best Chamber' and this, one assumes, must have been the equivalent of our present day lounge, the contents bearing this out – five chairs, six buffets, a square table, two chests and a box that was covered by a frame of sorts. But, Chamber could also serve another, much different purpose as was the case with that located 'Over the House'. Principally a storage room it contained some meat in arkes (chests) with domed lids while other arkes held some which had been salted. More 'chests' were lying around waiting to be filled. The presumption being that this room was used for the salting of to be kept meat (no fridges in those days), since also there is mention of nine barrells and a salting vat. And yet this room, too, must have been used as a sleeping quarter since in it were a trunkel bed and a quantity of furniture.

LIVESTOCK AND HUSBANDRY

The then given names of some animals may need explaining. A kine was a cow, young cows were heiffers while wethers were male sheep especially castrated ones and ewes with lambs were referred to as cupples. The Wainhouse was where wagons (waines) were kept along with husbandry gear (farming equipment). A fann was a basket used in winnowing grain etc. When considering the assetts and the liabilities shown on the inventory it should be borne in mind that £1 in 1692 had an equivalent value in 2006 of just over £90.

HANNETT HOUSE

One of the earliest references to this property I have stumbled across was in 1594 when one Philip Morton, having died, it was revealed in Sheffield Court that it also had adjoining land, a meadow, eight pigsties and a croft and they, we are informed, were divided 'by the waters of the Steyne within the soke of Bradfield'. Twenty-two years later a relative, Godfrey Morton, was living at Hannett House while in 1617 the owner was one John Beighton and he leased the house together with its outbuildings and land to a James Bagshawe. We leap forward now a hundred and forty-two years to June 7th 1759 when a 'Court Baron of the Most Noble, Edward, Duke of Norfolk, Lord of the Manor of Sheffield, met with his deputy steward, William Battie presiding' for the purpose of hearing a complaint being lodged by a Wortley butcher, Thomas Bromehead, and his wife, Katherine, together with a Sheffield Merchant, Samuel Shore of Norton Hall, about the bequest, made in his Last Will and Testament by Richard Bromehead, father of the first named whereby he left to Joseph Hawksworth, schoolmaster of the Low Bradfield school Hannett House and Hannett field. These were to be let at the most advantageous rent and the income derived therefrom was to be used by Hawksworth for the sole maintainance of the aforesaid school. The appeal was not allowed and so the children benefited. Once more the name John Woodhead comes into play here, because it was one of his twin sisters, namely Mary Woodhead, who became the first wife of the schoolmaster.

Fifty-two years later the property and its land were once again 'in the news' and this time they were the subject of a petition to Joseph Bishop, duly appointed commissioner of the 1811 Bradfield Inclosures Act by Thomas Marriott Perkins who submitted that he should rightly be allowed to retain no less than fourteen properties and land. Of these his eleventh listed was… "for my messuage called Hannett House… and all the buildings belonging thereto used and occupied and for all lands therewith usually or now held and containing about twenty acres and for all Toftf, Gardens, Orchards, Yards,

Fouldf, Plantations and Pleasure Grounds to the aforesaid Eleventh claim..."
How successful was he? Have a look at the outcome!

In 1864 Hannett House and its outbuildings were swept away by the surging
waters of Dale Dike Reservoir when its newly-constructed embankment was
breached and, of course, Hannett House land was totally submerged beneath
the waves.

THE WATERS OF THE STEYNE

It was past Hannett (oft-times referred to as Annett) House that from times
long past flowed the waters of the Styne, their source being the Moors way
beyond the top end of Bradfield Dale and into this ever widening stream was
fed the supply of many tributaries. In the thirteenth, fourteenth and fifteenth
centuries, Sheffield Court Records frequently mention the waters and name
them as either Strynd or Stryndes. At this point I gratefully acknowledge that my
frequent referrals to that ancient seat of justice have only been made possible
through consultation of Mr T. Walter Hall's 1926 published volume entitled 'A
Descriptive Catalogue of Sheffield Manorial Records'. The Oxford English
Dictionary informs that the meaning of Strynds or Strinds is a rivulet or a stream,
so such waters making their way down the dale were a vital necessity, (along
with supplies obtained from springs) for the drinking needs of the local
populace, for the watering of all beasts and for general usage about house and
farm. It has been recorded that between Thornsett and Low Bradfield there
were at least three holding troughs and ten springs at the beginning of the last
century.

THE MOORWOOD FAMILY OF 'THE OAKES IN BRADFIELD'

Before proceeding with the following notes one has to remember that there
were two ways of spelling this surname, Moorwood and (the older) Morewood.
According to Joseph Hunter's Pedigree of the family, Ref. MS 329 and pp80/1,
Ralph, a son of Richard Greaves, of Holdsworth Bank married 'Beatrice...
daughter of... Morewood of the Oakes', but I have never managed to trace
such a wedding taking place. What is recorded in the Bradfield Parish Registers
is a marriage between Raph Greaves and Beatrice Revell on August 27th 1593.
Some confusion here, one supposes, because in Pedigree numbers 464/465
this(?) Raph is shown as marrying Elizabeth, a daughter of Rowland Morewood!
Most certainly a girl by that name was baptised at Bradfield on March 3rd 1587
but her spouse was not a member of the Greaves family.

The Raph in question I presume to be Raph Greaves shown living at
Morewood and at Hopwood House, near Stannington. The Morewoods are
an ancient family and their name frequently appears in the Bradfield Registers
from their commencement, and from which point I will 'look-into' family
matters beginning with the residents of the 'Oakes' at that time, namely
Rowland Morewood, (a son of John) and his wife, Catherine (nee Stafford,
of Eyam).

19

Gertrude, sister of the aforementioned Elizabeth (and just five years after the death of Catherine) on January 12th 1601 married Jeffery Roberts. Two years later their daughter Elizabeth was born and when aged 29 she married John on August 12th 1607 baptised son of John and Jane Parker, of Jordanthorpe, the wedding being on July 9th 1632. Thirteen years previously at Bradfield her grandfather, Rowland Morewood was buried on July 1st 1619.

John and Elizabeth's great-grandson, of both Greystones and of Woodthorpe, in 1706 at North Wingfield, Derbyshire, married Mary, a daughter of Samuel Staniforth of Eckington and it was their daughter Sarah who married Sheffield merchant, George Woodhead of Highfields (more details later). Gertrude Morewood's brother Anthony, who married Frances Redhill, lived at Hemsworth in the Parish of Norton and their two children, twins, were baptised on July 16th 1615. One, Rowland, never married, lived at Alfreton, Derbyshire and died in 1647. His brother, Anthony, did marry and the couple had four daughters.

In 1635 the Morewood family living at Alfreton purchased from Lord Frecheville the ancient property at Norton known by the name of Hazelbarrow (house – farm).

Anthony and his children went to live there. In 1670 one of his daughters, called Elizabeth, married Henry Goring, of Lyndon, Sussex and so, through this union, the Hall and property passed to him. Interestingly, on June 30th 1697 John Woodhouse, of Midhope listed the lands owned by Henry Goring and these included the Midhope Moors and Commons where, as previously mentioned, the Wainwrights of Midhope grazed their flocks.

The original house 'The Oakes in Norton' is said to have been demolished in the 1670s and the present-day building was erected on the site in 1672, relating documents say that three years later the house was bought by a Joseph Morewood who, I am presuming, was the September 15th 1647 baptised son of Rowland and Mary Morewood, of 'The Oakes in Bradfield' and Joseph's brother was Samuel, the second son and who was baptised on April 2nd 1648. He married a Greaves, in the person of Elizabeth, the January 2nd 1655 baptised daughter of John and Gertrude, of Hallfield, the wedding taking place at Bradfield on July 13th 1675. Mary of course was her younger sister.

Samuel and Elizabeth had no fewer than seven children who were girls and just one son, John who, at Bradfield on March 7th 1689 was baptised. He was destined to marry twice. Martha, a daughter of Edward Kenion, of Holdsworth Bank was his wife No.1, the couple being married on 8th February 1716 and they were separated by the death of Martha in May 1743. It was another Martha, this time a daughter of Edmund Hancock, of High Peak who became John's second wife the following year.

Samuel and Elizabeth died and were buried at Bradfield on May 15th 1710 and July 2nd 1727, respectively. John Morewood, who is said to have been responsible for the sale of 'The Oakes in Bradfield', died on March 7th 1771 some seven years after the demise of his wife Martha. John's father, Samuel, was the great, great grandson of John, the first named (p464) Morewood in Mr Hunter's Pedigree of that Bradfield-based family.

'The Oakes' (overlooking Dam Flask) content

"The rambling old house of the Morewoods, called Oakes, overlooking Dam Flask, consisted, in 1715, of no less than seventeen rooms." Says D.J. Smith, in his 1987 published booklet 'Crafts of Old Bradfield' and in which we learn that (p8) in the 17th and 18th centuries they included "garrets, two butteries, two kitchens with chambers over them, a cellar and a dairy. This house was demolished in the mid-eighteenth century and replaced by a plain farm house." The husbandry gears at The Oakes were stored in the wainhouse, there also being a barn and a dog kennel, this latter evidently being used for the keeping of the hunting hounds therein. "Oxen, used to draw the encumbersome wooden ploughs used on the heavy land appear in Bradfield Inventories of the seventeenth and the eighteenth centuries, e.g. Samuel Morewood of The Oakes had two oxen valued at ten pounds in his inventory of 1715. Oxen were used to pull harrows, sledges and other implements. Slow, but reliable, oxen could be fattened and sold for meat whereas horses were simply worn out."

THE WOODHEAD FAMILY OF WOODSEATS (FARM)

Abraham Woodhead of Thwong, in the Parish of Almondbury near Huddersfield is said to have married Grace, the October 30th 1614 baptised daughter of Robert Ward presumably of Bradfield Parish since it was at Bradfield Chapel that she was christened. The actual marriage date eludes me but I feel confident that one of their descendants was John Woodhead, of Woodseats Farm. He married twice, his first bride being Mary, a daughter of John Fox, of Smallfield but only seven years were to pass after their wedding at Bradfield on October 28th 1675 before, at the age of 36, Mary died and was buried on June 26th 1682. No children are 'recorded' as being born out of this marriage but that really is questionable, in view of the following...

Mr Hunter's Pedigree for the Woodhead family shows John's second wife as Hope, and she was a daughter of Robert Clarke, the marriage taking place on October 11th 1688. In 1731 Hope married again and this time her husband was a man by the name of John Shemeld, of Grimesthorpe. In 1731, however, Hope (we presume) was a widow and that year she describes Robert Woodhead as "my son-in-law" so confirming that the Robert whose baptism at Bradfield, as a son of John Woodhead, which took place on April 25th 1677 could not have been her child but rather the son of John and Mary Woodhead.

Robert married a Mary Croydon on December 20th 1714 and the couple had three children. The first born, in 1717, Thomas, unfortunately died in infancy. Three years later on September 7th 1720 was baptised Mary while Dorothy was presented at the font on January 4th 1722. It was Mary, then only fifteen years old who became the wife, on November 30th 1735 of Thomas Marriott ('The Younger') of Ugghill while Benjamin Steade who resided at nearby Dungworth took Dorothy to be his bride on July 15th 1742 at Bradfield Chapel. So we know that there were Woodheads certainly at Woodseats Farm for at least one period of 60 years, continuously.

Woodseats Farm

But to refer back to the Grace Ward who married Abraham Woodhead. She had an older brother by the name of Robert and he, too, married a member of the Fox family of Smallfield. Doubtless related to the Mary who married John Woodhead, but of a previous generation the Bradfield Register of Marriages describes her at the time of the 1661 wedding as the 'widow Ffox' so was Robert her second husband? It is believed that they, too, lived for a while at Woodseats Farm.

Woodseats Farm – a description

At the time of compiling these notes I await a modern-day description of the farm and its outbuildings and such will be of much interest. Meanwhile, from some notes which Ida Smith wrote for the first volume of Bradfield Historical Society's publication 'Bygones of Bradfield' (p82) being very authorative upon the subject as applicable some eighty eight years ago I quote…

"I was born at Woodseats Farm in 1920, the eldest girl in a family of eight children, four boys and four girls. The large stone house was dated 1634 and had mullioned windows, some of which were blocked up, I presume from the days of the window tax. We had a large family kitchen with wooden beams. There was also a wooden seat under the window which could seat six children at meal times, and an old stone staircase leading to our bedroom.

"Outside were many farm buildings including a cruck barn which was in a fair condition when we left. We had 100 acres in a ring-fence at Woodseats with more rented land at Thornsett, so approximately 210 acres were farmed. We had a mixed dairy herd, 100 store lambs and three or four horses."

The water supply, apparently, for both Thornsett and Woodseats "came off the moors to filters in the wood until a ram was put in Agden to pump water to us."

Woodseats is shown/named by Jefferys in his 1777 'Map of Yorkshire' and the property also appears on the Ordnance Survey Map of 1855. Woodseats is mentioned by name sometimes in the Bradfield Parish Registers and probably the earliest of such is the September 13th 1577 baptism of Richard, a son of Richard Bacon.

The second volume of 'Bygones' also included (p22) some notes about Woodseats and this time contributed by David Robinson who informs that… "The Woodhead family lived at Woodseats until 1840. In 1841 Woodseats Farm was farmed by John Crawshaw and totalled 104 acres. In 1881, John's son, Jonathan had inherited and the farm was now 106 acres. The Shepherd family came to Woodseats about 1904 and lived there until 1979 when I moved in." Mr Robinson also speculates that Sheffield merchant, George Woodhead once lived at the farm… but we will deal with that later.

THORNSETT – THORNSETT AREA

The Jefferys Map simply indicates that Thornsett covered a large area whereas the Ordnance Survey Map shows both Lower and Upper Thornseat below Mortimer Road and on the bankside between this old Turnpike road and the reservoir. Starting on the opposite side of Mortimer Road and leading to Thornseat House, Thornseat Plantation, Thornseat Moor and Thornseat Delf (the site of an ancient quarry) was Thornseat House Road. To the left of this was the Bole Edge Plantation (Jefferys Map names this, latter as the Hallfield Moor) while, to the right that parcel of land was called the Miss Harrison Plantation and I wonder if it was so named because the owners were the sisters, Ann and Elizabeth Harrison, genealogically traceable to the 17th century family of Woodheads and the two ladies in question actually being they who were responsible for the building and opening of the Wadsley Parish Church in 1834 and in which adjoining graveyard the sisters are buried. People I have 'come across' living at or associated with Thornsett include...

1440   Appearance at Sheffield Court of John Greaves, on October 8th.

1529   Richard Day surrended a messuage at Thornesett.

1563   John Thompson held a messuage at Thornesett.

1591   John Thompson, at Sheffield Court, on April 8th was seised of land and a messuage at Mattockland in Thornsett. Interestingly, there were named in connection with this appearance his four daughters and details of their marital links with other families. Emot, for example, was the wife of Richard Bromehead, his kinsman Thomas Bromehead was the husband of Ann, while Elizabeth was the spouse of Richard Ibbotson whose brother I believe to have been William Ibbotson of the Middle Coombs Farm, near Oughtibridge. Finally, there was Diones said of late to have been the wife of Nicholas Stead and whose father, also Nicholas, of Onesacre had married either (1) Margery, a daughter of J. Ibbotson, or (2) Margaret Revell of Smallfield. If the latter then his bride was later to take to be her second husband Rowland Thompson, of Brightholmlee. The marriage of Nicholas and Diones lasted for some thirty-nine years until the demise of Diones in March 1619. There exists a belief, however, that she was actually his second wife because he is reputed, circa 1578 to have married one Agnes Shaw.

1587   This year living at Thornsett was a Henry Hawksworth because he was involved in Court proceedings regarding the surrender of a messuage called 'Dogehouse' together with six acres of land adjoining the property.

1615   The Greaves and the Bromehead families this year were to surrender and obtain a messuage lately used by George Woodhead, the 'move' being from William Greaves to Nicholas Bromehead, the gent who, in 1638 left his 'whole apparatus of beehives' to his three nephews. Honey in those days was a vital commodity.

1619   It was most likely that the Ellen Bromehead who married a Raph Greaves this year was a daughter of our aforementioned Richard Bromehead and Emot, his wife. The Ronksley family seemingly were living in the Thornsett area in the seventeenth century and I found a mention of Nicholas Ronksley, a Yeoman, in 1659.

1673   Saw the baptism that March of William Revell, of Thornsett, at
          Bradfield Chapel.
The surname Thompson appears to have been synonymous with such
          properties as Thompson House and Thompson House Farm in
          Bradfield Dale and for further enlightenment upon this point I did
          make local enquiries but no response was received!
1853-1856 Sometime during this three years period a Mr Sidney Jessop is said
          to have had built that property which became known as the
          Thornsett Lodge, it being sited upon land owned by and thus titled
          the 'Misses Harrison Plantation'. Other publications contain much
          information about this property so there really is little point in
          'copying' them here. During the 1940s the Lodge was used as a
          children's home for youngsters evacuated from Sheffield.

BEING WEAK IN BODY BUT OF SOUND AND PERFECT MIND

Such phraseology was almost invariably used during the 16th to 18th
centuries by those whose profession it was to write the Last Will and Testament
of many who for illiteracy reasons could not do so themselves. Therefore, what
was set down and legally sworn as being the product of a sound mind
contemplating death had to be and was acted upon. I ask you to bear this in
mind when reading extracts from two, very contrasting Wills which I include
since they form a part of the history of Bradfield. The first is that of Christopher
Morton and made on May 9th 1660.

One recalls that the Grace Ward who married Abraham Woodhead had a
twelve months older brother, Robert by name and he, on November 18th
1661 at Bradfield, married the 'widow ffox' and most probably taking her
as his number two wife as it is likely that he had been married previously
and from that union had been born two daughters who were called Mary
and Sarah.

The 'widow ffox' (Bradfield Parish Registers description) was actually Mary,
the February 11th 1618 baptised daughter of Christopher Morton of Wigtwizzle,
who was probably the 4th October 1573 baptised son of Richard Morton of
Wigtwizzle and so one of the beneficiaries of property by the Will of Henry
Gillott, and dated 1605.

When twenty-three, Mary, at Bradfield on December 24th 1641 became the
wife of John Fox, of Smallfield, he then being the twenty-five years old son of
Fulwood based Ulysses Fox. It seems that sisters married brothers because
Mary's sister Elizabeth became Mrs Stephen Fox, at Bradfield on April 7th 1650.
The couple had one daughter Elizabeth who died in 1679.

John and Mary Fox were blessed with four daughters. Ann married a Henry
Wood of Barnsley, George Wilkinson was the husband of Elizabeth, Sarah
(believed did not marry) and Mary whose husband was John Woodhead, of
Woodseats Farm. This latter couple in turn had three sons of whom two, George
and William, died in infancy. However, the third boy was given the name

William when baptised in 1648. He remained a bachelor and dying in 1672, left his estate to his four sisters.

Christopher Morton died in 1661, being buried at Bradfield on January 8th, some eight months after making his Last Will and Testament, he being 'weakened with old age', and also eight months after the death of his son-in-law and Mary's husband, John Fox. In essence he left all to be equally divided between his two daughters though he had reservations about interference from Ellen, his wife, whom he believed to favour one of the girls. It is a complicated Will wherein one detects a dislike of the person whom his daughter married after the demise of John (Fox), namely Robert Ward who (little did Christopher realise one supposes) was the supervisor of John Fox's estate. In fact, Christopher Morton stipulated that should Mary remarry then certain income should pass to her four daughters and to their brother, William, provided that he carried out certain details he was directed to do so in his father's Will. Elizabeth too, did not escape his strictures for if she failed to have any children then her mother was to distribute her portion of the estate to 'the right heirs of me, Christopher Morton' and which directive suggests that he had been married previously.

Ellen, his wife, was not overwhelmed with generosity because she was simply left a wife's 'rights' which, for example, in the case of Richard Spoone, of Stannington who had died in 1652 amounted to 'a seiled bed, a feather bed, one bolster, a mattress, two pillows, a pair of linen sheets, a couple of blankets and two coverlets along with half part of all moveable furniture, chattels and cattell'. One cannot imagine Ellen faring so well when the basics of those times following the demise of a husband was simply one good bed with some convenient furniture.

(One remembers that William, the older brother of John Fox married Ann, a daughter of John Morewood of 'The Oakes' in 1636 and after William died in 1648 Ann became the third wife of Henry Bulgay, an Attorney of 'The Hagg' in Derbyshire. It was from the marriage to his first wife, Grace Barber, a daughter of a wealthy sheep farmer, however, that Henry obtained a small fortune and some of this inheritance was used, it is said, to build Derwent Hall in 1673 not only for his own esteem but also to 'leave' to his son, Henry. The place was in constant use – its history really is most readable – until it was demolished in 1944 to make way, along with much else, for the flooding of the valley and thus the creation of the Ladybower Reservoir.)

The Last Will and Testament of George Woodhead, of the Highfield District of Sheffield, in the County of York, and of date June 2nd 1813

At the very outset it has to be said that this is an extremely lengthy document and in it there are, naturally, bequests to people who have no bearing upon our story but one has to bear in mind the testator was a very wealthy gentleman and merchant with premises in Sheffield and who had many friends and 'connections' in both the town and throughout the neighbouring counties. He is the person alluded to as having, at some time, lived at Woodseats Farm, Bradfield Dale, though not proved.

In truth, the certainty of his parents is not known but considered to be Joseph Woodhead, who, at St Mary's Church, Handsworth, on May 16th 1727 married Ann Crawshaw of that Parish. Joseph was a brother of the John Woodhead who, as already stated, married Elizabeth Stead, of Onesacre Hall, Joseph being born in 1702. The Handsworth Register does record the baptism of George to a Joseph Woodhead on November 12th 1732. One wonders if Ann Crawshaw was in some way related to that Thomas Crawshaw whom Gertude, the 1747 baptised daughter of John Woodhead took to be her third husband in 1801. Therefore, working on the supposition that the foregoing details are correct then George Woodhead would, indeed have been one of the grandsons of George Woodhead of Wigtwizzle and of Hallfield, where he died.

For those readers who wish to consult the original Last Will and Testament the same, and a copy, is available at the Sheffield Archives, Shoreham Street, Sheffield. From it I have obtained details of bequests to those who I thought 'fitted' or would come into our story about Bradfield Dale.

First, then, I have selected... "To the children of the late Joseph Wilson, an Optician, £100." Joseph was the 1745 baptised son of John and Isabella Wilson, of Fargate, Sheffield and Joseph's wife, Ann (or Hannah) was a daughter of Thomas and Sara Holy, of Sheffield. The Misses Ann and Elizabeth Harrison (owners of the Harrison Plantation) were Joseph's nieces and it was they who were to be responsible for the building, in 1834, of Wadsley Parish Church. George Woodhead, of Hallfield was Joseph's great grandfather.

To Miss Sarah Girdler, £100. She was related to the Smith family, of Cutlers, who lived in the Bellhouse district of Sheffield and it was one of their sons, William, who married Martha Eyre, of Worrall, Martha's sister, Sarah, became Mrs William Sampson and they lived at Worrall where, in 1690, a daughter, Sarah, was born. She married a John Greaves and the couple, who resided at Worrall Hall (look for the crest above the main doorway), were blessed with no fewer than eight children. One was the 1712 born Sarah who donated a substantial sum towards paying for the newly created Onesacre School, in 1797.

There were precious few bequests to members of the Ronksley, Hague and Crawshaw families and such omission created much exasperation since they were on George's 'side' of the family. Elizabeth Hawke, however, was an exception to this 'anti-Bradfield feeling' in George Woodhead's mind when he set forth his wishes. She, a cousin, was to receive the annual interest obtained from the selling of a parcel of land (which George Woodhead had purchased from the Duke of Norfolk) the figure realised being invested for this purpose. So it was also an indirect gift, I calculate for her husband too, Robert Hawke, since for years he had worked the 23 acres at Nether Bradfield. He also had much to do with the Onesacre School, in so much that it was he who sold to the Trustees a house, barns and some land in the Wigtwizzle area so that they could rent the same out and use the income derived therefrom for the benefit of the being taught poor children. The Trustees actually paid Robert Hawke the sum of £180 for this small 'estate'.

Elizabeth Hawke was a sister of Gertude and both were the daughters of John and Elizabeth Woodhead of the Woodseats Farm. Matters concerning Gertrude we will look at presently.

An executor of George Woodhead's estate was John Rimington and he was bequeathed the Greaves House estate in the Chapelry of Bolsterstone, such 'property' at that time being occupied by Thomas Milns. It comprised a house, barns, a cow house, stables and some land. Other members of the Milns family I perceive resided in and around the Worrall area and the two principal occupations of the menfolk were the manufacture of cutlery and stone masonry.

John Rimington's sister, Elizabeth Phillips, received £100. It was another of his sisters, Harriett, who married Rowland, a son of the Reverend Rowland Hodgson (a fellow executor) and Rowland Junior, benefited greatly from George Woodhead's generosity insomuch that he 'received' property and land at Red Hill, Crookesmoor, Brincliffe Edge, Heeley and at Newfield Green. Rowland had a sister by the name of Anna Maria and, to be sure, she was a certain favourite of the Testator's as is evidenced in both the 1806 Will which he made and that of seven years later which, naturally, cancelled out the former. The wording references to Anna Maria differ. In 1806 the Reverend Jonathan Alderson was Rector of Hornby and then George Woodhead decreed "Thirdly, I give and devise to my dear niece and adopted child, Anna Maria Alderson, the wife of my worthy friend, Mr Alderson"... while the 1813 version read... "I give and devise to my wife's niece Anna Maria the wife of my worthy friend the said Reverend Jonathan Alderson, Rector of Harthill and whom I call my dear adopted daughter..." the bulk of his estates amounting to some £60,000. The Aldersons had several children and one of them, Elizabeth, married sometime Clerk to The Company of Cutlers in Hallamshire, James Wilson.

Reference we said would be made to Gertrude, daughter of John and Elizabeth Woodhead, then of Hallfield. Her first husband was John Hague and their marriage took place at Bradfield on September 12th 1768 and they had a son, John. On November 13th 1771 as Mrs Gertrude Hague she married for a second time and now her husband was Isaac Ronksley. Their children included Isaac and Annis. Lastly, now Gertrude Ronksley she married a Thomas Crawshaw on December 30th 1801. The Ronksley family firmly did believe that George Woodhead's heir should be of their family and thus the bitterness about the contents of his Will, in which he refers to "John Hague son of my cousin Gertrude Crawshaw" also he must have been well aware of life in the Ronksley family some of whom, in 1806, were living at Hollow Meadows.

As to Anna Maria's inheritance which she was to have as hers, alone, "and to be disposed of by her and her heirs without the consent of her present or any future husband" the value could be calculated in 2006 as then being worth £35.63 for every £1 of 1814. Her 'gift' included...

> All his shares in the River Dunn Navigation Company and also those in the Sheffield Theatre together with his 'rights' title and interest in the Tontine Inn, Sheffield. All his estates, barns, stables, land at Killamarsh, his estate at Holdsworth in the Chapelry of

Bradfield (a house, barn, land) called Holdsworth Hall presently in the occupation of Jonathan Ibbotson, a barn and some stables at Loxley recently purchased from William Murfin and, rent-wise, producing £87 a year. Also, a farm at Bradfield by name of Smallfield and let to John Stocks at £40 per year and another farm at Bradfield rented-out to William Horsfield. In 1967 Smallfield was demolished. Interestingly in the 1806 version of his Will, Anna was also left an estate at Wadsley, bringing in a yearly rent of £35 from one George Armitage. She was also left 'a seat in Bradfield Church'.

George Woodhead's wife, Sarah (née Parker), had predeceased him by just a few months so the two houses they owned, including that at Highfields, also buildings, livestock, wagons, husbandry, furniture, plate, wines and liquers were to be sold and the money realised to be shared between brother and sister, Rowland Hodgson and Anna Maria Alderson and her son, Jonathan.

In his Reminiscences of Old Sheffield, R.E. Leader says (p256) that George Woodhead was initially an apprentice of George Greaves, a merchant who had premises in Norfolk Street almost opposite the Upper Chapel (and which person's son, George Bustard Greaves, was to become Lord of the Manor of Wadsley). When, one supposes, George Woodhead came of age Mr Greaves made him the offer of a partnership proving his satisfaction in his abilities but on the proviso that young Woodhead could find the sum of £1,000. This, we learn, he did by borrowing the amount from John Rimington, father of John, sometime Clerk to the Company of Cutlers in Hallamshire and henceforth the business became known as Greaves and Woodhead. When the senior partner died George Woodhead managed the business himself so effectively that he was able to have built a house at Highfields, somewhere between 221 London Road and Bramall Lane. Indeed, a road thereabouts was named after him. Unravelling the life, widespread activities and social circle the Woodheads were accustomed to is virtually like trying to complete some jigsaw where the number of pieces is totally unknown.

Last Will and Testament of the Reverend Jonathan Alderson of Harthill, made on July 5th 1847

Anna Maria, his widow, already wealthy from the bequests made by George Woodhead, received all Jonathan's land, houses and tenements in Yorkshire, Nottinghamshire and Derbyshire and after her demise such to be equally divided between son-in-law, James Wilson (who for a period lived at George Woodhead's former home, Highfields), her son Christopher, currently the Rector of Kirkheaton and, lastly, her eldest son, George. Anna Maria also received the linen, plate, printed books, china, furniture and pictures along with three milk cows, his two best horses and the chaise or carriage which they drew.

A Bradfield link next because £1,000 was left to his daughter, Elizabeth, the wife of James Wilson to be invested so that she could receive the income therefrom and after her death the capital to be shared between her children. One remembers that the East Window at Bradfield Church was given in memory of James and Elizabeth. Many bequests were made to other members of the family but they have no bearing upon our story.

Sugworth Hall (and cottage)

Snippets of information about this, said, Jacobean dated property, have been already published in other local history books so no point in repetition. I do have the sales brochure for the Hall when it was offered as recently as 1999 and it makes very interesting reading. A few more historical notes therefore will add to that which is known about this ancient and, for periods, family seat. Families known to have lived there include the Hooles and, of course, the Boots. There exists the Last Will and Testament of the 1560s occupier, Robert Hawksworth, though perhaps the premise is somewhat different now to that which existed in Robert and his family's days at Sugworth. He died soon after making his Will and the next head of the Sugworth branch of the Hawksworth family was his son, Henry, who is known to have been there, along with his mother in 1585. By an arrangement of 1612 made at the Sheffield Court the property and lands were in the tenure of Robert, Henry's son. Certainly, the Hawksworths were residing at Sugworth in the early 1630s. Eighty-eight years later it was the Goulds who lived at the Hall, for on October 16th that year was baptised at Bradfield a daughter, Mary, her parents being William Gould who thirteen years previously married a Mary Worrall. Bradfield Registers show that this William, however, was 'Junior' so perhaps his father was still alive. The Hall and cottage are Grade II listed buildings and, as such, they will be referred to later along with others mentioned in these notes.

What did become of Mary Greaves after her father died in the year 1692?

As already stated, with the demise of John Greaves his youngest daughter, then only 19, was left as the sole member of the family at the large house – Hallfield. Whether there were any servants living there we don't know. And, being under age, her guardianship had been undertaken by Woodseats farm resident, John Woodhead. Even so, did she wish to remain a maiden lady or did she have any ideas about matrimony since both her older sisters had married though one was living at Low Bradfield as Mrs Morewood, at 'The Oaks' farmhouse. Records never exist to tell us about these personal facts and the only way of trying to obtain such information is through perusing Parish Registers, or reading a family Pedigree, the last being the course I took and with some success for in that of the Greaves family compiled by Joseph Hunter (MS 329 p801) one does find just a few words which could point in the right direction and these are... "Mary G coh'r, under age 1692 (Q. if W. of William Fenton of Gleadleys, Gent?" Such a clue initiated much searching through the Parish Registers of Bradfield, Sheffield and of Handsworth and, eventually the entry was found in Sheffield's Record of Marriages that, on November 1st 1692 the marriage took place there between Maria Greave and Willos Fenton. This, I decided, must be our couple and I pondered if Mary had been doing a spot of courting while her father was still alive, or on the other hand did John Woodhead know about it? In fact the wedding took place only 149 days after John Greaves died, intestate. Again, one wonders if this was a marriage of true love or if William, who came from a numerous family, was an opportunist and believed that, eventually, there would be land and property coming to him as a result of such a 'convenient' union of the pair? The Fenton family had links to the Brights and from whence came Mary's mother, Gertrude. James Bright of Brincliffe Edge, married Judith a daughter of Alexander and Elizabeth Fenton of Gleadleys, and it is my firm belief that William was one of their descendants. So, once married, what became of Mr and Mrs William Fenton? The natural follow on in those times was the commencement of what often became numerous families with frequently at least seven or eight youngsters. It seems that William and Mary took up residence in the Fentons' stronghold, namely the vast Parish of Handsworth. Thus, a thorough search of the Handsworth Parish Register – actually it turned out to be a stiff-backed, feint ruled exercise book wherein, year by year in section sequence were entered the baptisms, burials and marriages at the Parish Church.

It would seem that the marriage lasted but two years and a half, if the details I obtained are relevant. On May 19th 1695 was buried 'Mary the wife of William Fenton', this was only months after "? son of William Fenton, Junior" was buried on 24th August 1694 and, even nearer to Mary's demise was the internment of Elizabeth, daughter of William Fenton, on December 24th 1694. So, did Mary die as a result of having the children? The date of Mary's death does tie-in with a document soon to be examined.

What did become of Hallfield?

According to Miss Greaves' notes published in 'Bygones of Bradfield', Volume No. 2, Hallfield was purchased, circa 1708 by Thomas Wentworth, of Wentworth Woodhouse and it, in turn, passed from him to firstly the Marquis of Rockingham and then to the Lord Fitzwilliam. This information probably came from the Wentworth Castle estate office. The Wentworth Woodhouse Muniment of deeds, correspondence, ledgers, account books and innumerable legal 'papers' comprise the vast collection held at the City Archives, Shoreham Street. To search through all these would have taken up a great deal of time, so assistance was sought of a kind employee (who no longer works there) and the result was that after a lengthy 'trawl' nothing 'concrete' could be found to confirm such a sale. However, all was not in vain. Far from it, because we stumbled across a document which related exactly what happened to Hallfield after 1698 – and this has the 'tie-up' with Mary Fenton's death three years previously.

It reads: "THIS INDENTURE made the Twentieth Day of April in the Tenth year of the Reigne of our Sovereign Lord William the Third by the Grace of God of England, France, Ireland… "Between Samuel Morewood, of Oakes in the Chapelry of Bradfield and County of York Gent and Elizabeth his wife and William Fenton of Gleadless in the Parish of Handsworth and County of York did (1) on the one part and George Woodhead of Wigtwizzle in the Chapelry of Bradfield, on the other part witnesseth that Samuel Morewood and Elizabeth Morewood and William Fenton… have demised, lett, leased all that messuage and tenement commonly called by the name of Hallfield with all the barns, stables, folds, yards, orchards, gardens, land, ground, commons, heriditaments together with one croft to the same known as Roger Croft, one house or tenement commonly called the schoolehouse all which said messuage, grounds… to have and to hold yielding and paying therefrom yearly forty pounds" and to be made in two equal payments at Whitsuntide and at Martinmas. George Woodhead covenants to carry out all necessary repairs to the property… "during the said Terms of Twenty One Years", so we now have confirmation that George Woodhead became the tenant of Hallfield in 1698 and from Wigtwizzle moving into the place very soon afterwards. The mention of a Schoolehouse is the first record I have seen confirming that such a place of learning did exist and therefore, it seems possible that the schoolmaster was 'housed' in the main house and thus the mention in the 1692 inventory of a 'Schoolmaster's Room'.

"One pillion seat, a fluskit and the small things she has anyway"

George Woodhead, of Hallfield and formerly of Wigtwizzle made his Last Will and Testament on December 29th 1740 revoking and making void all former Wills made by him. (One is believed to have been made on December 6th 1728). George actually died and was buried in January 1740 and his widow Elizabeth survived a further 16 years, presumably continuing to live with her son at Hallfield. Elizabeth was bequeathed "my cottage and croft at Thurgoland" also lands, messuages, tenements and crofts "lying and being at Thurgoland aforesaid during the rest of her natural life and immediately from and after her decease I give the said… to my son, John Woodhead and his heirs and assigns for ever."

"I give my dear and loving wife Elizabeth further one bed of her own choice and furniture sufficient to it one desk, one chest, one pillion seat, one fluskit and the small things she has anywhere about."

"I give my daughter Anne, wife of James Walton, fifty pounds. I give my granddaughter Hannah Newbould the sum of five pounds. Likewise I give to my daughter Elizabeth, wife of James Rimington, the sum of twenty pounds. Likewise I give to my son George Woodhead the sum of seventy pounds if ever lawfully demanded for his use and his children's otherwise to my son John Woodhead. I give unto each of my grandchildren twelve pence each. Likewise I give unto my son Joseph Woodhead my best suit of clothes. Likewise I give my daughter Hannah Wilson one guinea. All the rest and residue of my messuages, lands, goods, chattels, cattelles whatsoever and wheresoever after payment of expenses, dues and legacies to my son John Woodhead his heirs and assigns. I have set my hand and seale the twenty-ninth day of December in the year of our Lord One Thousand Seven Hundred and Forty and in the Fourteenth Year of the Reign of our Sovereign Lord George the Second King of Great Britain and so forth."

A few explanations

A pillion seat was a cushion-like seat which fastened at the back of the saddle to enable the transportation of a second person, the assumption thus being that George and Elizabeth regularly rode around together.

A fluskit was a tub wherein clothes were washed.

Granddaughter Hannah Newbould was an ancestor of the sisters Anne and Elizabeth Harrison.

Elizabeth and John Rimington's grandson, John, was the principal driving force behind the creation of the 1805 Sheffield Wadsley and Langsett Turnpike Road.

The recipient of the suit of clothes, Joseph Woodhead was, as we have discovered, the father of Merchant, George Woodhead.

What do we know about "My son, John Woodhead"?

Certainly that he was baptised at Bradfield on December 13th 1694 being the eldest of George and Elizabeth's three sons, his brothers being Joseph and George. Doubtless he would have been born at and spent his earliest years at Wigtwizzle before the family took on the lease of Hallfield in 1698. Educationally we don't know whether the brothers and sisters did receive any tuition from a schoolmaster or whether all they learned was from their parents.

If parish records are to be relied upon then John remained a bachelor for nearly fifty years before marrying, on January 26th 1743 Elizabeth who was the 14th May 1708 baptised daughter of Thomas and Elizabeth Steade, of Onesacre, themselves marrying in 1696 and Elizabeth (senior) being a daughter of Thomas Creswick, of Burrow Lee (Hillsborough).

John and Elizabeth actually married two years after George Woodhead's death and he must have renewed his lease of Hallfield which originally expired in 1718. His presence at that place in 1714 is certainly confirmed because, on 9th November conveyed to him by John and Ann Sanderson who lived at Whiston, near Rotherham were one moiety of a messuage at Brogging Ing, closes as Burgoyne Ing and the Byke Tree, for £70 per annum. It is believed that the above eventually 'came into' the hands of the Steade family since all the aforementioned together with a parcel of land at Hathersage and some property leased to John Hague at Grenoside came to John Woodhead as a part of the marriage settlement of 1743. John and Elizabeth had two daughters and one son, George, who died just twenty-five days after being baptised on 4th December 1744. Elizabeth, baptised on November 14th 1748 married Robert Hawke at Bradfield on June 11th 1770 while Gertrude, as has been previously noted, married three times. John Hague was her first husband (was he, I wonder, related to the aforementioned John Hague of Grenoside?) in 1768, three years later, in 1771, Gertrude became Mrs Isaac Ronksley. And finally, the trio was completed by her 1801 marriage to Thomas Crawshaw (again, was he a kinsman of the Ann Crawshaw who married Joseph Woodhead, she being the mother of George Woodhead of Highfields).

ELIZABETH WOODHEAD'S INHERITANCES

About four years before she married John Woodhead, Elizabeth's father, the wealthy land and property owner, Thomas Stead of Onesacre died and was buried at Bradfield on February 4th 1739 and by his Last Will and Testament he bequeathed to Elizabeth, apart from numerous 'chattells' the sum of £500 (the equivalent of which sum was, for instance in 2006, £44,250!) and another similar sum came her way just twenty-four years later, in 1763 and this time it was left to her by her brother Thomas Stead, also of Onesacre. But this time the money had to be invested by his executor and the interest only obtained annually was to be Elizabeth's for her natural life and thereafter the capital was to be divided between her two daughters. From all of this one gets the impression that John Woodhead, knowingly or not, certainly was destined to marry 'into money'.

"WHERE A VILLAGE STOOD, A WILDERNESS NOW APPEARS"

For safe keeping since it is irreplaceable and I must confess not read for many a long day in an upper cupboard at my home, is a handed down handwritten and beautifully illuminated copy of J.F. Shepherd, of Attercliffe's "Lines on the Bradfield Flood" and this copy through age and handling in its early years regrettably now is becoming 'brittle', cracked and the writing rapidly fading. But, before its does decay beyond repair I thought that for a little while you would like to ponder the lines, slowly and as we approach the sesquicentennial of the event in 2014 reflect upon that truly calamitous event. It is fitting, therefore, I believe to include the poem in its entirety as an 'In Memoriam' to those who lost their lives and as a recollection of what the power of water can do.

"LINES ON THE SHEFFIELD FLOOD"

Which occurred at Sheffield through the bursting of Bradfield Dam, between the hours of 12 and 10 o'clock on the morning of Saturday, March 12th 1864. When 798 homes were destroyed and abandoned, 4,357 flooded and over 250 PERSONS DROWNED.

The stars hung high o'er Loxley vale, the cattle sought the shed,
  The tiny stream danc'd gaily on, along its pebbly bed,
The sheep were gather'd in the fold, the bird had found its nest,
  And babes were nestl'd peacefully, beside the Mother's breast,

The strong man worn out with his toil, and children with their play,
  Had sought alike the sleep, that gives new strength to meet the Day,
And many a lov'd one and loving form had closed the weary eye,
  In slumbers never more to wake, or but to wake and die.

The cheerful lisp, the merry laugh, the cold or kindly word,
  Was whispered but in silent mien, and scarce a breath was heard,
Save but the wind, which at the close of day had been a breeze,
  That now had sprung into a gale, and whistl'd through the trees,
But HARK that strange sound, whence comes that DEAF'NING ROAR,,
  Like some stupendous avalanche dash'd on a storm tossed shore,
The pent up floods in Bradfield dale have burst the basin huge,
  And now comes thundering down the steep in one mad deluge.

And soon the streams became as brooks, the brooks as rivers wide,
  And the valley one vast sea, lash'd up by angry tide,
And furiously the bursting wave rushed through the ravine drear,
  DESTROYING ALL and everything that cross'd its dread career,
The sturdy oak, the towering elm, were snapped in twain like reeds,
  And ponderous stones borne high along, as ripples bear the weeds,
The bridges crumbled neath the....., the..... were torn and rent,
  And massive oak and iron beams, like twigs were writh'd and bent,
The farm, the homestead and the forge, the wheelhouse and the mill,
  And whatsoever man had made, of science and of skill,
The workman's hut, the rich man's stow, the wealth and toil of years,
  Were lost and where a village stood, a wilderness appears.

And high above the water's roar, was heard the voice of prayer,
  Man's agonising cry for help, his wail of wild despair,
For mid the wash of barn and field, the roots and trees uptorn,
  Swift on the billows surging breast, both men and beast were borne,
The aged matron, and the maid, the husband and the wife,
  The grandson and the infant babe, new struggling into life,
Alike were with the torrent swept, that from the dam now down,
  In one vast foaming cataract, overwhelming half the TOWN!

At length the day star's ray shone out, the night clouds drifted by,
  The sun rose calmly in the EAST and ting'd with gold the sky,
But what a sight that light reveal'd – what despolation dire,
  Enough t'appal the stoutest heart, and set the brain on fire,
Far, far as e'er could reach, sad evidence was seen,
  How strong and mighty was the flood, how fierce its rage had been,
So wide spread was the havoc, made, so vastly was the blight,
  IMAGINATION cannot paint the RUIN wrought that night.

St.Nicholas Church & Watch House, High Bradfield

From Bradfield hills to Bradfield Dale, Damflask and Malin Bridge,
  And along the green bank side, the Gorge, and o'er the Ridge,
From Loxley on to Owlerton, across and o'er Neepsend,
  And down the valley of the DON, in every turn and bend,
From Hillsboro' on to Harvest Lane, and the lowlands round,
  Along the Wicker and its ways, where'er a path was found,
The huge uproarious sea had work'd its devastating track,
  ENGULFING all within its reach in universal wrack.

Uprooted trees, logs, bales and beams, great heaps of bricks and stone,
  And mighty engines ripp'd and crack'd, like toys about were thrown,
A thousand beings homeless made, upon the damp ground stood,
  PALE, shivering in the cold MARCH wind, knee deep in slime and mud,
And o'er the waste of sludge and mire, stern men in bands were spread,
  Close eyeing every chink and nook – the searchers for the DEAD!
And children for their fathers wept, and fathers for their sons,
  And mothers scarcely mothers made, wept for their little ones,
The widow mourned, the husband lost, the husband mourned the wife,
  And everywhere was heard a WAIL for loss of human life!
Thus perish'd nigh three hundred souls beneath the boiling wave,
  For tho' Men heard their cries for help, Man had no power to save.

O Man!, how vain thy boasted skills, how feeble is thy power,
  To HIM who can the work of years, destroy in one short HOUR,
To thy ambition, Sheffield lays this elemental strife,
  This wide expanse of misery, and fearful waste of life.
But while a throb beats in the heart, or mem'ry holds her throw,
  GOD, grant the like Calamity, may ne'er again be known.

J.F. Shepherd
Attercliffe.

THE PARISH CHURCH OF ST NICHOLAS, HIGH BRADFIELD

So many references have thus far been made in our notes about Bradfield Chapel and more are in the 'pipeline' that I considered just a few notes about what became St Nicholas Church, at High Bradfield would be appropriate, without plagiarising the excellent histories compiled by other, local historians – see later.

Bradfield, of course, is one of the places where you will still find a small building close by the church and which was constructed for the sole purpose of acting as a Watch Tower or Watch House and from within whose walls could be kept a constant surveillance of the church burial ground for at one period such a last resting place was the target of the unscrupulous person, who, for a 'consideration' was quite prepared, mostly when it was dark, to visit a graveyard and without the slightest compunction disinter a newly buried body, cart it away and deliver the same to a medical school where research purposes would be the objective. Such a stealer of the dead was called a 'body snatcher'. Within this graveyard were laid to rest many of the people already mentioned in our look around the Dale, probably both baptised and married there. In the times of which I write the place of worship was a Chapel of Ease to St Mary's Church at Ecclesfield.

Between the very first, in 1490 and the present day there have, I reckon, been well over forty ministering priests at Bradfield and of them the one I found to be of so much interest was John Hoole (you remember he married Ann Marriott, of Ugghill in 1659) who was appointed the same year to care for the Souls in the Chapelry. In my notes about the families concerned with the early days of Underbank Chapel I have included much about John's activities. It is a fact that only three years after taking up his duties at Bradfield he was displaced because of his non-conformity. Whether he resided with the Marriott family is not known during the four years following his suspension but it seems he must have had a change of heart (or been persuaded) and reversed his opinions thereby allowing him to be reinstated to the Ministry of Bradfield Chapel in 1666 and at which he remained the priest until 1701.

A couple of references, only, I promised. There they are and the rest of the history of St Nicholas Church and also a guide as to what you will find both within and without I recommend reading before making a visit of an unhurried nature to the church, of the perpendicular style with its pinnacles and Gargoyles, embattlements too, and having spent a while quietly 'drinking in' the past happenings at this ancient place of worship venture out into the adjoining churchyard and spend some time looking at the many weathered, leaning headstones, some bearing a name now familiar to you. Mention of graves reminds me that, in his Last Will and Testament, Richard Spoone of Stannington directed that, in 1652, every poor person attending his funeral was to receive a dole of three pence each. One wonders how many took up the offer?

The booklets to consult are:

    A Little Guide for Visitors, compiled by then Bradfield
    Churchwarden and Feoffee John C. Wilson about 1969
    and
    A History and Guide "Researched and Written by
    John and Julia Hatfield" in 2004

TOUR ROUND THE DALE

Of course, it naturally follows that having spent an interesting time at St Nicholas Church then a gentle perambulation or a leisurely transportation round the Dale would be excellent so that you could espy, even at a long distance many of the places and areas of land taken as our subjects, and perhaps before doing so a little repast at one of the hostelries in the areas may prove quite refreshing. One ancient property which, until a few years ago, was for a period a beer house and a public house, is to be the next place we shall visit on our look around this scenic district.

THE HAYCHATTER (HECHATTEN HOUSE)

In endeavouring to arrive at a date when the earliest messuage was built at, and naming the then occupants of Haychatter, in the Chapelry of Bradfield it is essential to remember that the records held there of baptisms, marriages and burials only commenced in the year 1559. Therefore, what follows is based upon details extracted from such records, fragments of information obtained elsewhere and assumption that I have 'got it right' but always welcome any suggestions as to correcting. It is true to say that, over the years quite a number of inaccuracies have been found in the Chapel Registers. As a matter of fact some years ago I managed to trace a descendant of that Robert Hawke who sold his Wigtwizzle property to Onesacre School and this particular gentleman, who died in 1825 and was a Church Warden at Bradfield between the years 1799 and 1802, also able to 'read, write and do arithmetic' actually had the job of overseeing the making of correct entries in the Chapel's Registers. All that said, what do the pages reveal?

On 1st August 1568, at Bradfield Chapel, Elizabeth Bramall and Thomas Broomhead were married. We do not know how old both were nor have any details about parentage since such information was pre-register days. The first child to be baptised on July 10th 1569 being a daughter, Anne. Allowing some twenty years for further siblings then there are recorded twelve, and they were five boys and seven girls.

Since the Baptism Register did not record the name of a child's mother it is quite possible that, of those twelve some may have been parented by the Thomas Broomhead who married Genet Broomhead at Bradfield on July 19th 1574. Forty years later the youngest of the dozen, Emot, who was baptised in 1589 would have been 25. Probably many married after spending their childhood and their youth exactly where, home-wise?

Wills of the period are of little help since they only state a locality and within the Chapelry, not a specific house, messuage, farm. As we already have discovered there were numerous mentions of Broomheads living at Thornsett (Thornseat) but exactly where as the name applies not only to one of the old Divisions of the Parish of Bradfield but also to a couple of areas at either side of the more recent Mortimer Road. On one side there were Thornsett Delf, Thornsett Moor… whilst opposite were Thornseat, Upper Thornseat and Lower Thornseat.

One has to hazard a guess and I would say the latter group were the likely location of the family. The year, 1614, I mention purposely because then, ageing (about 70) and thus becoming all the weaker, Thomas Broomhead had to arrive at a decision as regards Haychatter where one presumes he, his wife and second son, John were then residing. But, with other members of the family expecting to benefit from any bequests after their father's demise how to satisfy everyone? After careful thought he had his wishes set down and witnessed by independent people, not immediately related. He so chose as to the property that the matter had to receive official sanction and that is why in the year mentioned one finds in Sheffield Court proceedings:

"1614 September 8th Sheffield. Small Court held there... At that court it was presented and found, that on 6th February then last Thomas Bromehead of Bradfield out of court by Henry Bromehead and William Saunderson, surrendered etc the east end of one messuage with a parlour and a chamber (cum conclaui et camera), then in the occupation of Richard Birley and called Hechatten House; to the use of himself Thomas Bromehead for life, with remainder to John his second son for life the same John paying yearly during the term (of his life) to the heirs of his father Thomas the yearly rent of iid, holding of the lord etc; and the rest of the messuage aforesaid with a small croft to the same belonging and its other appurtenances; to the use of him Thomas Bromehead for life; with remainder to Elizabeth then his wife, for her life, she paying yearly to the heirs and assigns of Thomas iiiid and to the lord rendering rents and services etc."

It seems, therefore that the property was owned by Thomas and his intention was that after his death (I believe this took place in 1616, he being buried at Bradfield on April 24th) his son John and his wife should then continue to live at Haychatter on the proviso that they paid a yearly rent to his heirs and assigns, the assumption being that they were his other children, but were they? Notice, "then his wife" written into the document. Does this imply that Thomas had been married previously? It's worth considering because John, following his parent's marriage in 1568 was legally stated to be the second son of Thomas. So, who was the first and when was he born? Taking all things into consideration, of those times, there is an entry in the Chapel's Register of Baptism of one Robert, son of Thomas, christened on August 24th 1567. Of course the name of his mother is not recorded. He lived for five years, but if he was the first son then John would have been the second.

ALSO WAS CALLED THE HAYCHATOR

Another spelling of the place name is shown in the Burials Register in 1709 when on September 15th Reginald Bramall, junior, of Haychattor House, and a son of Reginald Bramall, was interred. Baptised on April 1st 1684 he was just twenty-five years old. With the marriage link between the Bromeheads and the Bramalls perhaps the Haychattor was included in a marriage settlement and passed from the former to the latter family.

But, to return to 1614 and the mention then of a part of the messuage being in the occupation of Richard Birley. Who exactly was he? Genealogically the most likely person would have been that Richard, a son of John Birley (Burley) of the family who resided at 'The Yews' at Worrall, Richard at the time being aged about 36. The Burleys in turn were linked to the Marriotts of Ugghill by at least one marriage, being that of Mary, daughter of Edward Burley of 'The Yews' to Joseph Marriott, a grandson of John Marriott, of Ugghill, the last named having taken Ellen, a daughter of Raph Greaves of Hallfield, to be his wife.

Certainly the messuage/farm name was unusual but when we think about it very much 'in tune' with that all-important happening, each year, in and around the Dale – harvesting, haymaking. The 'chatter' of those employed in gathering in the hay, corn, barley, wheat would have been natural and so this could have formed the second part of the name, the first being taken from any one of the 'cereals' being harvested. Traditional methods, mostly dating back to the Medieval times were used to 'bring in the harvest' and 'tis said that for a four to five weeks period each year most of the villagers would be employed in the work (most useful to augment their meagre incomes, anyway) and at the conclusion of which it was customary for the farmer(s) to invite all who had helped to a great, harvest supper where there would be much joyous activity, food – home prepared – galore eaten and huge quantities of home-brewed ale consumed. What a vast difference between those times and the gathering-in of 2008.

Details of listed buildings in the Bradfield area include mentions of floors being used for threshing purposes in several Cruck Barns and the process used. Yes, I think we can agree that Haychatter was a good choice. We'll come back to the 'house' presently for its history was not just about farming but also the homely atmosphere of being, for long, one of the local public houses.

Not only did Thomas Marriott Perkins petition the Commissioner in the Bradfield Inclosures of 1811, for the retention of his Hannett House and also all the buildings etc., belonging thereto but he also appealed for the keeping of... "two, certain Fields called Rye Acre and Little Meadow, formerly part of Haychatter Farm and containing about six acres...

"and a certain Field or Part of a certain Field formerly part of Haychatter Farm and then called the Poole but now a part of a certain other Field called Horsley and containing about one acre....

"My messuage called Haychatter and Haychatter New House and all the buildings thereto belonging used and occupied and for all lands therewith usually or now held and containing about 20 acres and all tofts, gardens, orchards, foulds, yards, Plantations and Pleasure Grounds to the aforesaid Twelvth claim belonging or herewith held all which aforesaid Twelvth Claim is in the occupation of myself and are in the Township of Bradfield and Parish of Ecclesfield and are Freehold."

Why were they his?

Lots, which it isn't proposed to 'delve into' could have happened since we last found in 1709, that Reginald Bramall, junior, had died at Haychatter. However, as regards property coming into the possession of the Marriott family of Ugghill, much was held by 1660-born Thomas Marriott who, in 1685 married one Sarah Shawe but within months of the union he had died. There were no children and the estate, which he had inherited from his grandfather, John Marriott, was left to his file-cutter nephew, Thomas Marriott who, we recall, had in the year 1735 married Mary Woodhead, of Woodseats Farm. This marriage lasted some 19 years until Thomas died in 1754 leaving his wife 'well looked after' but the estate passed to his brother, Benjamin Marriott who, in 1749 had taken to be his bride a member of the Worrall family in the person of Hannah. Once more there were no children so by his Last Will and Testament of October 23rd 1761 Benjamin left his estate "by default" to "my kinsman, Thomas Marriott Perkins son of my nephew the Rev Jonathan Perkins upon the condition that he makes Ugghill his place of abode." Benjamin's great uncle Joseph Marriott was he who had married Mary Burley while his great, great grandfather was the Ugghill-based John Marriott whose wife was, of course, Ellen, a daughter of Ralph Greaves, of Hallfield. Family connections, galore!

(I omitted to mention that the Lord of the Manor of Sheffield in the year 1637 levied a rent charge on Haychatter of just 1½d or in 2006 say 5s. 0d.)

CAME THE DAM BUILDERS

For a very long time farms, mostly mixed and of varying sizes along with small holdings there had been a-plenty in and around the Dale and all, naturally, vying with each other for the necessary custom needed not only to keep them in business but also to bring in sufficient funds to cater for the, in many cases, every increasing number of children being added to the household. Therefore, it comes as no surprise to find secondary employment absolutely essential and so the farmer may well have milked his cows and then become a part-time cutler and produce a few knife blades. Or he may have sold his services to a neighbouring farmer and helped with lambing... The labourer would have eked out his living costs by doing all sorts of menial tasks such as wall repairs, hedging, ditching, mucking-out.

And so, one supposes, this traditional way of life in the tranquillity of the Dale carried on until one day the local populace had a very rude awakening with the news that the Sheffield Water Committee had made the decision to utilise the area for reservoir building in the late 1850s and for the construction of four reservoirs – Damflask, Agden, Dale Dike and Strines in the 1860s. What that involved can be read elsewhere. But the immediate impact on those who for generations past had lived in the area intended for flooding must have been devastating since they had no choice but to seek pastures new and see their ancient homesteads wholly or partially demolished and the land they had used, cultivated, simply submerged beneath millions of gallons of water.

Commencement of the work, of course, brought an influx of men, some being craftsmen of a particular trade while many were navvies who were used to working on such major projects. Irrespective of the tasks they undertook the work was hard, back-aching, strenuous and doubtless the builders were mighty glad of a rest at the end of a day's toil. So what better place to go than into the 'local' for the consumption of some strong, locally brewed ale and food with it. The chance for relaxation, socialising, a game of draughts, chess…

Naturally, such demand did not go unnoticed in certain quarters and the idea quickly came to mind, 'why can't I supply the requirements of those chaps?' And it is precisely that line of thought which, I believe, prompted the then occupier of the Haychatter to augment in no uncertain way his farming income by opening up a part of his farmhouse to sell beer and where, too, many a weary bone could be rested before a welcoming, crackling fire and the beer gently supped, probably with a Ploughman's meal. It is said that the sale of ale was brought about by demand from the local quarrymen but such can hardly be true since there had been quarries in the Thornsett area for quite a long time anyway and presumably those who wanted to enjoy a tankard or two would have gone to other public houses either at High or at Low Bradfield.

So, it came to pass but exactly when is not known and trade we suppose flourished. Many things were to happen at, and concerning, the Haychatter during the next century and a half and for those who seek such detailed information it is to be found elsewhere. Suffice to say, for the purposes of this exercise that during the period the beer-off eventually became a Free House, the place and farm building were sold several times, there was a frequent change of Landlord and the name of the pub was changed to appropriately the 'Reservoir Inn'. With completion of the work on the 'dams' in the 1870s quite a sizeable amount of trade would have disappeared from the hostelry by the departure of those working on the construction of the water-holders. And so custom then had to solely rely on the passer-by, the hiker, perhaps locals living close-by. With the passing of time it was inevitable that the pub receipts would gradually lessen. However, the 'Haychatter' continued to offer friendly, homely hospitality and a good pint of ale… until its closure was brought about by the death of the last landlady, Mrs Margaret Elizabeth Siddall, who passed away in July 2003 at the age of 77.

THE MYSTERY OF THE BROGGINGS

BROGGINGS – a strange name indeed, and one which presents quite a conundrum. I have tried to resolve its meaning and present my findings for your consideration, but it would be very interesting to have the ideas of readers upon the subject. If you 'split' the word into two parts then the 'ing' is quite simple because it means a movement, as in… walking, cycling, reading, pondering… It is the Brog which does present a problem. Learned scholars have expressed their views and here are some…

The Reverend J. Bosworth, Ll.D. in his 1838 London-published Anglo Saxon Dictionary has nothing for Brog, but Broga means… fear, dread, horror, trembling and even a monster.

Henry Sweet, M.A., Ph.D., Ll.D., in his Dictionary of Anglo Saxon words, published some sixty years later also has nothing for Brog, but offers Bogen, a plant; Brogn, a branch or twig; Brogden, a sword. Can't think of any of those fit, so what does the Oxford English Dictionary tell us? Here we do have explanations of Brog including the fact that a brogger was a broker, agent, jobber.

Perhaps that might give us a clue suggesting the occupier of such a named premise was one who was prepared to arrange a deal, perhaps a 'short-cut' especially when one bears in mind that William Shakespeare's father, John, a glove maker by trade was not averse to purchasing the wool he needed by negotiating through a brogger with a shepherd or flock owner to purchase his needs and thereby avoiding the 'cut' which would have had to be paid to a merchant. By conducting his business in this manner it is said that John had a quicker 'turn round' and speedier despatch of his gloves to markets. Incidentally, in those times of the sixteenth century, gloves were made by glovers locally at Stannington, Holdsworth, Bradfield and Worrall, though one inclines to the view that they were more of the leather type, probably some being gauntlets. There again, of course, there were animals aplenty in the areas concerned and whose skins, after being slaughtered were processed by the local tanners.

In previous pages we have already recorded Brogging was a place name for such a named messuage which was leased in 1715 by George Woodhead, Senior. Probably this small property existed a hundred years previously and is that recorded in the proceedings of Sheffield Court of January 23rd 1616 when a William Green (not Greave) of the Holling House (Hollingdale) surrendered the messuage to Nicholas Broomhead. Here it is also recorded that Green had, himself, obtained the property when it was surrendered to him by Richard Carr.

We already know that George Woodhead took on the lease of one moiety (a half-part) of a messuage at Brogging in 1714, together with the Burgoyne Ing for a yearly rent of £70 (an Ing is a plain, even piece of ground, maybe a meadow).

Who had occupied the messuage before that time I have not discovered but there seems every likelihood that George Woodhead went on to purchase the messuage otherwise it seems highly unlikely that the owners would have permitted him to have his, and his wife's, initials inscribed into the stone lintel over the central doorway. Actually this part of the property is mentioned in the full details of its official listing, under reference 8162 – SK29SW, and where one reads that in the 20th Century a new central door was fitted. Brogging is described in one word: 'Farmhouse. GEW. 1718 on lintel'. The G.E.W. being George and Elizabeth Woodhead. The property, not given a century dating, was said to have been constructed using 'coursed, squared gritstone'. It was two storeys high, had '3 windows to the first floor' and remedial work had been carried out on the chimney stack.

Where exactly is the place? The Ordnance Survey Map of 1855 shows it at the very end of that lane which passes Hallfield and divides the Coo Hill Plantation on the right and the property called Stubbing on the left, likewise Brogging. On the opposite side of the lane and adjoining the Coo Hill Plantation is an area of meadowland called the Brogging End. To the right of, and traversing the Coo Hill Plantation is the Mortimer Road and on the opposite side of it there is located the Bole Edge Plantation.

Looking carefully at the map it would appear that in those days proceeding along the road would (as, indeed now) bring one to the ancient Strines Bridge. Then a left turn took one presently to the Strines Wood and the Strines Public House, some 1,015ft above sea level whereas another road seems to start at the bridge and it is called Foulstone Road. Probably a better description would be a Bridleway. However, proceeding along the same at its very commencement one passed on the left the Fox House Plantation while on the other side of the 'way' was the Brogging Moss Plantation. Immediately behind this and of some considerable area was the Brogging Moss itself extending towards Howden Edge and Cartledge Stones Ridge. Mystery here again because it contained the Brogging Moss Grotto! The Moss must have been an extremely damp, boggy place for one can count on the map at least 16 noted springs many of which fed into the Foulstone Dike and so entered the Strines Stream eventually passing into the Dale Dike somewhere in the proximity of Brogging 'house'.

GAME HAD SOMETHING TO 'GROUSE' ABOUT

For how long this area of moorland beyond Bradfield had been a breeding ground for grouse is not not known but the customary sport of shooting the birds down while in flight seems to have had its beginnings sometime about the 1840s up to when the shepherd's role was infinitely more important than that of the gamekeeper. Shooting Butts were unknown!

In August 1845, the owner of some 1,654 acres of grouse shooting moors in the Derwent, Moscar and Strines area, namely John Read, decided to try and sell his acreage by auction in three lots and these were only a small portion of the moors of the Bradfield Game Association. But, despite a 'glossy' picture being presented of the region in question there were no sales and offers were well below the reserved prices. Even the assurance that the acres were 'abundantly stocked with black and red grouse' held no sway.

The above information was included in a very lengthy article by G.H.B. Ward in the 1934/35 handbook of the Sheffield Clarion Ramblers and entitled 'The Story of the Derwent Road', and here the writer described these moors as being "intersected by springs and brooks and presenting every variety of moor which forms the resort of the grouse. The picturesque River Derwent nearby 'affords fine trout and grayling fishing'."

The most recent, 2006 edition of the Ordnance Survey Explorer Map (OL1) of the Peak District Dark Peak Area also shows Brogging, Brogging Dike, Brogging End, Brogging Moss Plantation and, whereas not included on the 1855 map, now one finds both on the Foulstone Moor and the Brogging Moss sides of the Foulstone Road a number of Shooting Butts.

Well, now, having assimilated all the foregoing, having harked back to the contents of the original Grants for Grazing & Co and thought about the area,

45

add a few more pertinent words – Dike, Ditch, Boundary, Wild Boar, Hog, Breed and Rushes – and, dear reader what conclusion do you arrive at as to how the name Brogging came into being? For myself, and as a starter guess I think it has some bearing in relation to the early Charters and the use of them for grazing sheep, cattle and even thereon letting loose geese. As a Forrester had been appointed in the early days did he have a successor who kept an eye on, regulated, controlled this – maybe other – areas(s) and he being an Agent (brogger) who lived in the house provided with the job, namely Brogging? What ideas have you? I have put out a few feelers for more information particularly about the occupiers of the messuage and we shall have to wait and see if there be a response. If so I will gladly inform you later.

FROM WIGTWIZZLE TO WINDSOR

When I first set out on this project I had simply no idea that the enormous amount of research would bring with it several extremely nice bonus stories which I will share with you, and the first of these takes us through from the Wigtwizzle area to the Frogmore Estate adjoining Windsor Castle, one of the homes, of course, of the Royal Family. To avoid repetition I will take as my starting point the major beneficiary in the Last Will of George Woodhead, of Highfields and of Norfolk Street, Sheffield, a Merchant, being Anna Maria Alderson, his niece and said adopted daughter. A grandson of George and Elizabeth Woodhead, originally of Wigtwizzle, George died in October 1813 just a few months after the demise of his wife Sarah in June and a sister of whom, Mary, was the mother of Anna Maria.

While he was serving as the Rector of Langton in Swaledale the Reverend Jonathan Alderson became Anna Maria's husband when they married in 1795. Some seventeen years later the couple moved south to Eckington in Derbyshire the living of which Parish Mr Alderson had accepted and where he continued to minister to parishioners until his death in September of 1848.

He was the first born son of the Rev Christopher Alderson and his wife, Elizabeth, who had married at Aston on November 25th 1767. Christopher being the son of Jonathan and Elizabeth Alderson, of High Ewbank in Westmoreland, and aged 30 at the time of his marriage to Elizabeth. His mother Elizabeth was a daughter of William and Elizabeth Ball, of Aston.

In fact, William was the Steward to the members of the Darcy family who resided there but whose ancestral home was in the Holderness area and which place they took to their title when a forbear was awarded an earldom. The Darcys had lived at Aston since the reign of Queen Elizabeth the First. The Pedigree(s) of the family make interesting reading but, for our purposes, we will take as a starting date the year 1719 when to Robert Darcy, the Third Earl of Holderness was born a son whom his parents had christened, not surprisingly, Robert. He was to marry a lady by the name of Mary Doublet about the time that he held the position of being a Lord of the Bedchamber to His Majesty, King George III.

The first two appointments that Christopher Alderson had after his ordination to the priesthood were at Howgill, in North Yorkshire and at Langton in Swaledale. In 1784 the Aldersons came to Eckington when Christopher took up the Rectorship of that Parish and which Ministry he continued until his death in 1814. During a part of that period some time was spent assisting at All Saints Church, Aston, where he became the Rector in 1797 following the death of the Reverend William Mason who had served the Parish and its people for no less a time than forty-three years. A native of Hull, he studied (though not necessarily for the Ministry) at Cambridge where he was awarded a Fellowship of St John's College.

Nothing really is known about his studies for Holy Orders, though following his ordination in 1755 when aged 31, he was offered the living of Aston by Robert Darcy then the 4th Earl of Holderness.

In 1761 William Mason married a much younger lady but only seven years later she died and for the remainder of his life the Rector was a widower, but, apart from his ministry he pursued his two great loves, poetry and gardening, the latter and the neighbouring countryside being the subjects of his sonnets and verses. In fact he was referred to as the Poet of Aston. He was a great friend of Thomas Gray whose own works include the famed 'Elegy written in a Country Churchyard', and the two often exchanged visits to one another's homes. The Aston Rectory garden was designed and laid-out by him and it featured flowers, tulip trees, bushes, irregular walks and arbours, all of which he kept in first-class order.

Mr Mason had been dogged by ill-health for some years before he died and to help with the parish duties Mr Alderson assisted in the role of curate. Doubtless, the two perambulated the garden frequently and some of the enthusiasm of the elder priest must have been 'passed' to the Eckington Rector although, truth to tell, perhaps he was a keen gardener himself already. He too planned the garden at his home and maybe it was quite an eye-catcher. So much so that, unbeknown to him his prowess did not go unobserved by no less a person than one who knew him already, being Mary, now the Dowager Countess of Holderness who continued to live at Aston despite her role, in the late 1780s as a Lady of the Bedchamber of Queen Charlotte.

In 1790, Her Majesty had taken the lease of a then farmhouse at Frogmore, about half a mile South East of Windsor Castle and being interested in matters botanical herself she wished to quickly have a start made on the land attached to the farm. And whose help did she seek?

(Here I have been privileged to have the generous help of the Royal Archives at Windsor Castle.) Writing, in February 1791 to her son the Duke of Sussex, the Queen told him that... "Lady Holderness did recommend him to me and sent him to Windsor. I have begun to plant the 7th of this month and from thence I date the beginning of my little paradise." Princess Elizabeth, one of his sisters, also wrote to the Duke saying that she and others "came to Windsor as usual last Friday and this morning has been employed in a very pleasant way to me as I had the pleasure of seeing Mama very happy at the arrival of Mr Alderson, a Yorkshire clergyman. They staked out a walk this morning." The Queen thought Alderson "a man of great natural taste but not of the world."

Work went apace on the cottage garden and in 1791 Queen Charlotte bought, and had much altered, the farmhouse. 'Frogmore Palace' as she was pleased to call her new residence overlooked a lake she named her 'ornamental water'. And here, too, major work was undertaken by both Christopher Alderson and by her Vice-Chamberlain, William Price, with the creation of canals, serpentine walks, mounts, glades, bridges… the plants, bushes and materials to be used were chosen by the Queen, who originally had commented that Mr Alderson had "undertaken to render this unpretty thing pretty."

I am informed by Windsor Castle that "Although there are no letters surviving to or from Mr Alderson in the Royal Archives there are occasional references to his work." Also that "it is uncertain how long Mr Alderson carried on working at Frogmore but work continued for some years."

(The foregoing is only a shortened version of the 14 pages of handwritten manuscript "From Wigtwizzle to Windsor" and this original has been accepted for use and reference in the Windsor Castle Archives. I was informed it "contained some very interesting facts. It is particularly interesting for us to have some background on the Reverend Christopher Alderson who appears in our records only in connection with the gardens." (The letter of acceptance, signed by Mrs J. Kelsey, Deputy Registrar, The Royal Archives, Windsor Castle is dated the 22nd of December 2006). The second of the 'bonus' stories obtained from the undertaking of this 'look around' I will relate presently.

RESERVOIR STATISTICS

Fancy writing about Bradfield Dale without providing a few basic statistics concerning two of the Reservoirs which the walker, traveller will surely pass. Both supply drinking water. The farthermost, Strines, covers some 55 acres and its deepest point is 67 feet. With a holding capacity of 453 million gallons, it was constructed in 1869. The Dale Dike Reservoir we view is, of course, the second on the site as its predecessor, when filling ready for use in 1864, rapidly emptied with disastrous consequences when on March 11th/12th the retaining embankment burst open and the vast amount of water it was holding back simply poured out and went thundering down the valley, through Low Bradfield, Loxley, Malin Bridge and Neepsend. The present 'dam' which holds 466 million gallons of water, has a deepest point of 67 feet and covers some 62 acres, was constructed in 1875.

LIST OF BUILDINGS OF SPECIAL ARCHITECTURAL OR HISTORICAL INTEREST

"The middlestead of the barn was always kept clear for here the threshing was done later in the year when it was too wet or cold for outside jobs. The threshing was done with a flail… (which)… was made of very tough wood like holly or blackthorn," the handle being of ash. "The handle had a swivel on its top and the swingel was attached to it by thongs of snake or eel skin, the underside of a horse's tail or sometimes just pigskin. When using the flail the thresher swung the handle over his shoulder and brought down the swingel across the straw just below the ears so that the grain of corn was shaken out without being bruised."

"While threshing was going on the big double doors were pinned back; as also was the smaller one in the opposite wall. The through-draught thus set up helped to carry away the dust. Then followed the sieving. Grain by the shovelful was thrown into the air and the heaviest fell farthest away while the lighter dropped short, and this was usually used as cattle feed."

The foregoing, which appears in his Faber and Faber published 'The Fellow Who Cuts The Hay' (London, 1956) was written by George Ewart Evans and it gives meaning to just four words which form a part of the Official Listing details comprising that for the cruck barn at our oft-mentioned Woodseats Farm at Windy Bank. Seemingly the building was inspected way back in 1975 and the structural content it was decided merited a Grade II classification. Believed constructed in the 17th century 'of Gritstone rubble, with a stone slate roof', of 4½ bays with 'outshot on left' and having 'a cart door with buttress on right, and cow house door with wooden lintel to far right. Rear former cart door mostly blocked. Three cruck pairs rising from above floor. King post truss to right and cart doors remain'. The Listing Reference is SK29SW, 8/124 and being of date September 20th 1975.

According to the Reference No SK29SW, 8/123, it was on February 25th 1952 that the Woodseats Farmhouse was granted a Grade II Listing in view of the many, both internal and external features considered to be of great interest both to local historians, architects and to antiquarians.

As a read-through is bound to do, it makes one wonder how many of the items currently 'listed' actually existed when the farmhouse was occupied by the members of the Ward and the Woodhead families? When constructed it is believed that the same Master Mason was responsible not only for Woodseats but also, though differing slightly, for Hallfield and Onesacre Hall too. View them and you can see the similarities. Of course, with all Listed properties it is always best to visit the Central Library, Local Studies section and very carefully consult the Listings yourselves.

They are contained in the Department of the Environment Book, City of Sheffield – Peak District National Park, South Yorkshire. The Parishes of Bradfield and Ecclesfield and the Township of Stocksbridge. Within those pages you will find much more, for instance, about Woodseats Farm than I have selected for our notes.

It has mullion windows, dripmould, a gable frontage, corniced ashlar sandstone and arched fireplace openings. The property was built of ashlar sandstone and has a stone slate roof. Of three storeys in height the farm has, above a rear window the inscription and date 'R 1631 W'.

LOWER THORNSEAT FARMHOUSE

"Formerly listed under Lower Thornseat" we are informed and having as its reference SK29SW 8/28 this property is described simply as a "Farmhouse. Door lintel inscribed AW 1721" and like many other buildings in the region it was constructed using "coursed squared gritstone (with a) stone slate roof." It is of a "two room plan with partial outshot extended to continuous outshot. Two storeys, three first floor windows. Doorway to left of centre has quoin reveals and deep lintel all chamfered". Lower Thornseats Farmhouse was given a Grade II Listing, it would appear on February 11th 1976.

HALLFIELD HOUSE

Our oft-mentioned house received its official Listing on October 21st 1974 and, again it was classified as Grade II. The usual reference applies, being SK29SW, with the number this time being 8/63. Described as a Farmhouse, the earliest part is dated as "Mid. C17 with later additions and alterations. Deeply coursed and squared gritstone and slate roof. Rectangular plan, with gabled entrance front and rear wing rebuilt 1977. Three storeys with attic, four bays…" One feature, I must confess, I thought quite delightful and I pondered how many generations of small children must have gazed up at it and, ponderingly asked their parents to tell them why it was placed in a "ground floor room to right a C17 plaster overmantle of lilies and roses under frieze of fish, fruit and mermaids playing harps, with cornice." Many, many more features are listed but such would occupy much space.

SUGWORTH HALL

Likewise, the Listing details for the Hall are numerous and so I have selected a few but for those who wish to read the entire details then the reference for Sugworth Hall is SK28NW, 12/104, P9678 but of unknown date. A Grade II classification has been given to the Hall. It is described as being a "Farmhouse now country house C17 core extensively reworked C19, with C1930 tower wing, probably by E. Vincent Harris, for Charles Boot.

Coursed, squared sandstone and gritstone, the earlier work of superior finish, some later-work herringbone-tooled. Stone slate roofs, ashlar stacks. L-shaped C17 range with hall wing to right and crosswing to rear projecting to left, the angle infilled, and with tower to rear right. Two storeys with three-storey tower. Panel above (entrance front) carved with lion and crossed hatchets and the motto 'DEO NON FORTUNA' under dripstone. Tower to right has embattled corner with well-dressed oriel balcony, two-canted bay with mullion and transom windows to rear, and flat roof. Interior; C17 hall: sliced spine beam indicates position of baffle entry against former smoke hood and heck wall, and correlates to door in right wall. C20 wing attached to rear left corner of range not of special interest."

In his 'A Glossary of Words used in the Neighbourhood of Sheffield' (London, 1888) Mr Sydney Oldall Addy informs us that in the Last Will and Testament of the Archbishop Rotherham, latterly Archbishop of York, and carefully prepared over a period of eighteen days (6th to 24th August 1498) mention is made of Sugworth; "Vole quod praedicti Johannes et Ricardus habeant tenementum mean vocatum Sugworth in parochia de Bradfield" and this would indicate that in the late 1400s two of the local inhabitants of Sugworth were a John and a Richard, but their surname is unknown since the Archbishop (about whose ancestry very little is known) did not include this information in his Last Will and Testament.

ONESACRE HALL

If the listing for Sugworth was lengthy then that for Onesacre Hall is more so. Strictly speaking, not within our area but mentioned in the booklet, I have devoted much space to this ancient seat and the Stead(e) Family who, for generations did live there in my notes about the early days of the Underbank Chapel and also in the publication 'Roads to Worrall', but in neither was I able to include the details of the property listing so I make amends here. Grade II* classification was given to Onesacre Hall and as the items are so numerous I recommend that you examine them at the Central Library where they are to be found under the reference of SK29E, 9/37 and of date 25th April 1969. It appears that the Hall was "formerly listed as Tophill Farmhouse, Onesacre" and according to S. Jones in his study, 'Houses in the Vernacular Tradition in North Yorkshire', (published in the Archaeological Journal, vol. 137 of 1980 and pp386/7) it is a 'Large house, now two dwellings. Two builds, C1630/40 and C1660/70'. I give just a few details and they are that construction was of "Ashlar sandstone except left return which is bedded rubble, stone slate roof. Modified H-plan, only left cross-wing projects to rear. Gabled. Two storeys and attic. Five windows to first floor, double chamfered mullion windows throughout, some transomed. C20 leaded casements." And many interesting features follow including "Wing to left with a large projecting stack terminating in twin corniced flues. Interior; chamfer-stopped beams in wing to left. Rich bead moulds to hall and wing to right which also retains a large arched kitchen fireplace in the rear room. Shallow projecting stone fireplace in hall." Judging from a glimpse of the Stead(e) Family Pedigree it is easy to understand why it became necessary to carry out extension work. The assumption, of course, has to be that there was a house of unknown size on the site, or thereabouts from early times because the Stead(e) Family are known to have been at Onesacre since the early 1400s. In 1625, it is recorded that at the (?former) house/Hall were Nicholas and his wife, Frances (née Beighton) along with their son, Thomas and two daughters, Emote and Jane. Thomas was to marry Gertrude Broomhead and in turn their son, Nicholas, took to be his wife one Mary Milner, in 1669. There followed the births, between 1672 and 1690 of eight children, namely Thomas, William, Mary, Elizabeth, Nicholas, Sarah, Jane and Anne. And, as time passed by, the number of members of the family remained either similar or on the increase.

WIGTWIZZLE TO WASHINGTON

I promised to reveal a little something about a second 'discovery' which I made absolutely by accident when compiling notes upon another subject, and

51

then it was about some of the historical buildings and the land upon which they stood in the very heart of Sheffield. To do so demanded much perambulating of the City streets and it was in the course of doing so that I frequently used the shortcut between Pinstone Street and Norfolk Street, namely Cheney Row, that alleyway which 'runs' between the Town Hall and the Peace Gardens. But, Cheney! I thought that the name sounds familiar! Curiosity prompted me to begin an investigation and I discovered that the naming had its origins in the fact which happened in the early 1720s, when the piece of land between the then recently built St Paul's Church and where now is Chapel Walk was purchased for less than £100. One imagines that it was a speculative move since houses and workshops were eventually built on the land where, in the late 1800s, was constructed the Town Hall. The purchaser was an Edward Cheney of Halkin and of Bakewell, Derbys.

Next, I thought, some research into the Cheney family may prove interesting and so it turned out to be. With much generous help from many sources I managed to trace them back, through numerous generations, to Raph De Caineto and his wife, Maude (nee De Waterville) who were living in Ashford, Kent, in 1086. Once settled there, having arrived from the Continent following the Norman invasion they soon set about making links with other families and how successful they were. Through the Sandys family of The Vyne, near Basingstoke a trace was made to Winston Churchill while the Lascelles who built Harewood had marital ties. Then there were the Howards, Cavendish and Manners families (the Dukes of Norfolk, Devonshire and Rutland, respectively) included in the Cheney 'expansion' which even extended to a relationship to an Archbishop of Canterbury and an Archbishop of York. They were indirectly associated with the Gunpowder Plot and a trace through has been made to the well-known Disney Family. We must not forget, too, that the Cheneys were connected by marriage to two of the wives of King Henry VIII, being Anne Boleyn and Katherine Parr. A trace of the 'branch' created in America following the emigration there in the early 1600s of Lawrence and his family led me to, and an expression of interest has been expressed by the present Vice President of the United States of America, namely Richard Herbert Cheney.

HANNAH CADE, EDWARD CHENEY AND THE WOODTHORPE ESTATE

But, to return to matters local. In 1724 at Bakewell Parish Church, Edward Cheney married Hannah Cade, a spinster, to whom – having described her as his Kinsman – John Woodrove, of Woodthorpe by his Last Will and Testament dated September 10th 1719 bequeathed the major part of his vast estates both at Woodthorpe and elsewhere around Sheffield. One ponders, though, if he took her age into account when he stipulated that the gift was for her to enjoy for the rest of her natural life and following that the estates were to pass to her 'begotton' sons in order of their age. Now Edward Cheney, who was indirectly related to Hannah must have heard of her exceeding good fortune but not known of the proviso that the sons of Miss Cade should be next beneficiaries.

Married once already he must have considered that here was a real 'plum' and so the wedding took place one assumes more for that reason than for 'true love'. Well-past child bearing age when she married, at 59, Hannah is known to have been living at Woodthorpe with Edward in 1728 but afterwards she just 'disappeared', Edward gained nothing from his 'investment in Woodthorpe Estate' and married for a third time. John Woodrove directed that should there be 'default' and the absence of any sons then the estate was to pass to his Kinsman John Parker, and so it did. And here we have a marital link going back to George and Elizabeth Woodhead of Wigtwizzle and of Hallfield the grandparents of George Woodhead, of Highfields who, one remembers, married Sarah, a daughter of the John Parker who received the inheritance. For those of our readers who are interested in reading fully the story I obtained about the trace-back then my manuscript, entitled 'Portobello to Pennsylvania Avenue' is in the City Library, Local Studies Dept.

WALKER HOUSE FARM AN ANCIENT PROPERTY ALSO

Listing details there are not for Walker House Farm but it would seem safe to say that, construction-wise it is of the same period as Woodseats Farm, Hallfield and Haychatter and a few items of information I have about the property I propose to list datally. In 1565 at the Sheffield Manor Court of George, sixth Earl of Shrewsbury and held on August 7th, Henry, the son and heir of Robert Hawksworth, was questioned as to why without the "leave of the Court, in contempt of the said lord and against the custom of the Manor" he had "demised and granted to farm... a messuage and two closes of land (called Mattockland) in Hawksworth Hed, called Walkeden House to Ann Hawksworth his mother to hold to her and her assigns for ten years without fine with the lord..." Word of this 'gift' must have reached the ear of Earl George and so Henry was seized of the messuage and two closes and as a punishment they were offered to anyone else who wished to take them. The only response, and that for their return, came from Henry and so he was permitted a continuity of them. It would seem that the messuage and land had, earlier in the year been "surrendered" for Henry's use by his father. The Henry and Robert, in question, were the father and son mentioned in our notes relating to Sugworth, Robert's wife being Ann and Henry's grandfather Henry and his wife, Joan, were both living in 1513.

Difficult to imagine now but in 1565 Earl George was just three years away from marrying Elizabeth, Lady St Lee ('Bess' of Hardwick) as her fourth husband while in 1570 he was given the task, by Queen Elizabeth I of being custodian for the following fourteen years of Mary, Queen of Scots at the Manor (Lodge) a task which was to create much jealousy of his wife.

Our next date is January 5th 1613, when at Sheffield Court half an acre of land at Nether Tofte in the soke of Bradfield was surrendered to, and for his use one John Hawksworth, of Nether Bradfield by Thomas Hawksworth of Walker House.

A few weeks before his death, Thomas Hawksworth surrended on April 15th 1618 a messuage called Lodeshouse and several closes thereabouts and at Ugghill Woodside recently purchased from Michael and Ann Burton and presently in the occupation of Robert Hawksworth and John Smithe, to the use of Robert Hawksworth of Sugworth. Thomas Hawksworth was described as a Yeoman and living at Walker House in the Chapelry of Bradfield.

For the year of 1638 the rent charged by the Manor authorities for Walker House was 3s 8d payable at Martinmas and 6s 11½d due at Whitsuntide.

I have as next date, by year, 1754 and that was when James, a son of Francis and Martha Ronksley of Riveling Side married Sarah, a daughter of Thomas Hawksworth of Walker House, Chapelry of Bradfield.

Several claims made by Thomas Marriott Perkins for his properties and land in connection with the 1811 Bradfield Inclosures Act have already been related. Here was another and this time Mr Perkins described Walker House as "My Mansion" whereas the other homes were simply messuages. He also listed all the usual Tofts, gardens, orchards, folds, yards, plantations, pleasure grounds... and declared that Walker House was currently occupied by Thomas Gregory who, himself, had numerous sub-tenants, etc.

Then there was the occupier some years later with the strangest job... and what about... I am afraid activities at, names of future residents and matters relating to Walker House (Farm) after this period are being deferred in the hope that the pleasure of revealing the same may occur at a later time. Then, also, will be addressed other omissions in the booklet and namely the Agden area, Tenter Bank, the Upper Hoyles Farm.

THE WORRALL FAMILY AND STRYNDS

In the 'Yorkshire Notes and Queries' Magazine, Vol. 11 of 1906 was printed a most informative and illustrated article about Bradfield Church, written by the Reverend Arthur Briarly Browne, M.A., who by that year had been Rector of the Parish of Bradfield for eighteen years. His 'Notes' included a love(ly) story, dormant for nigh on 350 years, but whose background was just 'waiting' to be discovered!

"Some few years ago," wrote Mr Brown "There was remaining at Strines a pane of glass with the interesting legend inscribed with a diamond, in beautifully clear xvi century hand: 'Oh! Ye charming Mistresse Dorothy Worrall', a testimony to the excellence of the fair daughter of the house from an admirer, John Kynge by name and no doubt of whom we read in the old register, 1562: 'John Kynge and Dorytye Worrall maryed the xx1 Day of February'. This interesting memorial fell into the hands of a member of the family from London who was visiting the home of his ancestors and who is expected, should these lines meet his eye, to send for such a piece of vandalism a handsome donation towards the restoration of the Church." Actually, from the commencement of 'The first volume of the Bradfield Registers, comprising the years 1559 to 1669 inclusive 'in a parchment book, well bound in leather' Kynge-Worrall Weddying was the thirtieth to be entered therein.

The Worrall Coat of Arms

But, what exactly is known about the couple? John, it appears, did not live in the Bradfield Parish area. His is the only surname, Kynge, to appear in the aforementioned registers which, Parish-wise would include Bolsterstone, Stannington, Oughtibridge, Loxley, Worrall, Ugghill, Sugworth and very near to Derwent.

A search for the surname, Kynge in the Registers of St Mary's Church at Ecclesfield proved negative and sparse, indeed, were the Kynges to be 'found' in Registers of St Peter and St Paul, Sheffield and St Michael the Archangel at Hathersage although there I did come across the baptisms and marriages of some members of the Worrall family, but from where did they come? Locally based or maybe from Strines since that place is, more or less, equi-distant between both Bradfield and Hathersage and so, from the family point of view either of the parishes would do for Christenings and weddings.

But, it was in the most unexpected place that I met with, hopefully, success. It would seem that Dronfield or thereabouts was the home of John Kynge and I am of the opinion that there was a definite link between Dorothy and John's 1562 Bradfield marriage and the following entries in the Registers of the Parish Church; Dorytye, baptised on 18th July 1563, Christopher on March 1st 1571, William on November 11th 1574 and John on June 6th 1577 and all were shown as the children of John Kynge (no mother's name, of course, was recorded). Perhaps, I pondered doing a 'trawl' through the Registers of St James Church at Norton, the aforementioned Dorothy was she who, when aged 30 married one William Allen on November 5th 1593 at Norton?

From extracts of both Dronfield area Wills and entries appearing in the Holmesfield Court Rolls it appears certain that the Kynge family had, since the 1600s, lived in the Holmesfield and the Cordwell Valley areas and that they were much involved in sheep farming, breeding. Witness the fine imposed in 1499 upon a John Kynge of 12 pence for failing to keep his sheep fold in good repair! Another John Kynge, by his Will made some forty three years later bequeathed to his son-in-law 20 wether sheep. About this time the Kynge family also had a 'shepherd' among their number and he was called William. This reverend gentleman also had a son called John and when his father died he received Dad's best jacket and best doublet.

In the 1550s a curate of Holmesfield Chapel was called John Murray and he 'left' to a Mr and Mrs John Kynge, Senior, clothing and bedding. It seems the priest also had a few sheep and in his Will he dirested (if same be lawful?) that – being looked after by a Christopher Kynge – as and when they (and lambs) were sold then the proceeds were to be used towards the upkeep of the Holmesfield Chapel.

The question is, with so many Johns around who was the father (and mother) of the John who married Dorytye and the same had to be said also for her. Indeed, how, when and where did the young couple meet in the first place? The common denominator is that the farming, rearing of sheep was the principal business of both the Worrall and the Kynge families so, maybe, the introductions were made by the parents. From that time romance blossomed...

HOW OLD IS THE STRINES INN?

Following, for Listing purposes, an inspection of the Strines Inn about forty years ago it was decided to award a Grade II classification and under the familiar reference of SK29SW, with number this time being 9/69 and of date April 25th 1969 the salient features were... "Public House. C17, C18, C19. Coursed and squared gritstone with ashlar wing to left, stone slate roof. Elongated range of three builds, two C17 bays with two bay wing to left, brought forward and single bay wing to right set back. Gabled porch right of centre with ashlar surround to doorway, cornice, shield of arms of the Worrall family, kneelers and copings. To rear of C17 part, three light double chamfered mullion window with hood, mullions removed. Cast-iron benchmark on roadside gable."

Be the experts correct then the earliest part of the present day building not having been constructed until sometime post 1600 this presents a quandary as regards the aforementioned pane of inscribed glass. Date wise it has to have been in existence at least forty years prior to commencement of building work to 'tie-in' with, or perhaps before Dorytye and John's marriage. Which begs the question 'was there a messuage, description unknown, on or near this very same site pre-1600?' If so, then we can imagine, being delighted with their future son-in-law's much pleasing gesture Dorytye's parents allowed the "charming" pane to be fitted in some prominent place in the house for all visitors to see (and agree with?). Now, if when the first part of the 1600s build took place it incorporated that part of the former home wherein the glass was positioned then it would have remained there until, as Mr Browne explains, it was removed by a descendant of the Worrall family. If a former house was demolished to make way for the C17 home then the pane would have automatically been transferred. But, just supposing the Worralls were not at Strines at the time of the marriage where did they live? One has to bear in mind that the inscription did not make any mention of Strines. Puzzling, but essential to get locations.

THE WORRALL FAMILY AT UGGHILL

The very earliest person I can trace living in the Ugghill-Edgefield area and having the surname Worrall (probably originally Wirhale, or the likes) was in the late 1400s when I came across both father and son with the Christian name of John. In 1517 a William Worrall made an appearance at the Sheffield Court when he surrended to his wife, Elizabeth, and their two daughters, Ellen (who married a John Hall in 1570?) and Alyce (the bride, in 1574 of Thomas Batley?) some property and land at Hawksworth and to be shared equally between them. Dorytye seems to have been a girl's name very rarely used by the Worralls anyway, and the sole occasion I can find it at Ugghill was when a daughter so christened was the April 1580 child of Richard and Margaret Worrall. Alas (but common in those times) the little one only survived for 15 months. Henry was an oft used Christian name both at Strines and at Ugghill.

I am inclined to the view that it is one such, of unknown parentage, who was a brother of 'our' Dorytye and who, by the year 1562 had become the father of several children, one of them being christened Dorytye! Possibly one of Henry's sons, of like name, married in September 1599 Grace Hawksworth of Thornseat while another member of the Worrall family, John, took to be his wife one of the Hawksworth girls, again called Grace, and that was in October, seventeen years previously. Another link between the two families came about in 1627 when, by License, and on July 23rd, at Bradfield, another Henry (perhaps he baptised in 1602) married Ann Hawksworth. Five years later was born their son, Henry, and his grandson, Henry, married twice. His first wife in 1687 was a Susanna Heyld but she died in 1690. The second marriage took place soon afterwards, to a Martha...(?) but she, too, was by her death in 1698 to predecease by many years her husband who died at the age of 83 and was buried at Bradfield in 1743. It is believed that both Henry and John's families for a period lived together at Strines. One of John's children was Grace (born in 1589) and she married a John Machon, the youngest son of Raph Machon, of Hallom, in November 1613. His father and his older brother, Robert, in an out of (Sheffield) Court settlement, presumably as a gesture/part of a dowry surrended a cottage and two crofts for the couple's use, the agreement being witnessed by Thomas Hawksworth, of Walker House. There appears to have been a continuity of marriages between the Hawksworths and the Worralls for I find them again, in 1598 (Ann Worrall and Robert Hawksworth) and on August 28th 1687 (Robert Worrall married Ellen Hawksworth). The Worralls also had matrimonial connections with another well known family, the Revells. Remember that the children of Henry had by 1562 included a Dorothy! I wonder if it was she who became the wife of Richard Revell, in September 1583? A hundred and twenty years later Anthony Worrall became the bridegroom of one Mary Revell, said of Townfield Head. Could it have been their descendant, Anthony Worrall – whose wife was Ann (née Stringer, of Hathersage) – who in 1751 received payments from Bradfield Chapelry for "trees felled on Mr Worrall's land at Strynds with boughs cut off and the trunks" and duly transported to High Bradfield where used, "for the scaffolding for the pointing of the church".

TRADE PROVIDED BY THE TURNPIKE ROAD

By the time of this Anthony's death in 1776 much progress had been made on the construction of the Mortimer-inspired Turnpike road leading from Hathersage to Penistone and routed via Langsett. Before that date the section between Moscar Farm and just beyond the bridge(s) at the bottom of the steep hill beyond Strines going towards Bradfield had been completed. Surmising the almost certain possibility of trade, a stop for refreshment by the stage coach travellers or, better still, maybe an overnight stay is considered the reason why Anthony Worrall decided to turn part of the ancient house into an Inn with much accommodation available upstairs. The ale was home-brewed and the sign of the Bull was erected near to th e main entrance of the Inn. Once more we are reminded that our newly, self-appointed 'host' did not intend to rely solely upon customers entering his hostelry. Oh no! The very long standing family tradition of sheep rearing carried on with, at the time of his demise, no fewer than 355 sheep roaming and grazing on the nearby moors.

By 1776, too, the several hundred years' occupancy of the ancient family seat was swiftly drawing to a close and the Worralls would disappear from that locality. New 'blood' was to arrive at the pub with the installation of the first landlord, 'outside' the family and, as Directories and other publications reveal, there followed a series of them. An old document relates that for one period the name of the Inn was changed to the Taylors Arms and all sorts of reasons are given for the alteration.

While strictly speaking just a little beyond our remit, geographically, of the Dale I feel sure the Inn and the Worrall family played no small part in the day by day goings on by their immediate neighbours, thus the lengthy inclusion of matters pertaining to Strines I feel is well justified!

Many of the families mentioned in our notes were of such social standing that they had their very own Coat of Arms and these are still to be seen at some of the homes or, of course, in Bradfield Church. One thinks of the Rimingtons, the Morewoods, Hawksworths, Bulgays, Greaves, Marriotts and, naturally those for the Worrall family so finely carved over the principal doorway. But, dear reader, the range of the spectrum is mighty and here, people wise I find it so very sad that while those of the members of families we have 'looked' at and many others we haven't were much privileged and finely inscribed headstones are theirs in Bradfield churchyard, those of lesser means lived a much grimmer life and no marker stands above their grave. This was forcibly brought to mind not only at Wadsley Parish church but also elsewhere. For example could the following be much nearer to 'home' with our subject? From 'A Pocket Guide to Superstitions of the British Isles', by Steve Roud (Penguin Books, 2004) I read: "A widespread and persistent belief, reported from the mid-sixteenth to the late-nineteenth century, held that the northern section of a churchyard was unsuitable for the burial of respectable Christians, and should be reserved for strangers, paupers, suicides, excommunicated persons, the unbaptised, and stillborn babies. It thus took on a sinister and 'unlucky' reputation and often remained mostly unused for centuries. 'I asked the sexton at Bradfield why, in a churchyard that was rather crowded with graves, there was no appearance of either mound or tombstone on the north side? His only answer was, "It's mostly them 'at died i' t' workhouse is buried att' backside o' t' church" – Yorkshire (1851). And how far away was Bradfield's workhouse from its Chapel/Church?

THE HOLLIS HOSPITAL AND HARVARD UNIVERSITY

"BY DEEDS dated the 26th and 27th August 1703, Thomas Hollis, the Elder, citizen and draper of London, conveyed unto Thomas Hollis his son, John Hollis and 11 other Trustees and their heirs a building called the Great Hall or New Chapel, in Sheffield, near to Mill Sands, then converted into 16 small apartments and some dwelling houses adjoining, in trust, to place 16 poor persons of the town of Sheffield or within two miles round the same in the apartments…"

So one reads (p3) in 'Hollis Trust – Some Historical Notes' by E.H. Harrison (2003) and he provides details of the creation of both the Hollis Hospital and the commencement of a school for fifty children where "the boys" are to be taught "to read and the girls to read, knit and sew" in a room adjoining the main building.

Thomas Hollis, the Elder, was to marry twice. Mary Whiting, of East Ham in Sussex was his first wife while his second choice just happened to be Anne, a sister of Robert Thorner, his friend and one who, like Thomas (a Baptist), was greatly interested in matters educational.

In 1638 John Harvard, a Puritan Minister whom both knew well died leaving a half of his modest estate to be used for the establishment of, and all his library books to be available for students attending an intended College to be constructed at New Towne (Cambridge), in New England.

Much impressed by this venture Thomas decided that he wished to contribute to the foundation and he became a benefactor. Through his generosity two endowments were made. The first was a Fellowship in Divinity and the second was the creation of a Professorship in Mathematics and Natural Philosophy.

Successive generations of the Hollis family continued to support the College until the early 19th century, not only monetarily but also by periodically sending packing cases full of text books.

But what, you may well enquire, has the above to do with Bradfield Dale?

When he was 20, Thomas was considered so proficient that his 'Master' released him from the final year of his apprenticeship in the making of cutlery so that he could go to the Capital to manage a shop selling (much to the annoyance of the London cutlers) goods made in Sheffield by his 'boss' namely John Romsker who, that relationship apart, just happened to be his uncle and to whom he first went to be tutored in 1648. Success attended his managerial duties and presently Thomas decided to diversify into selling other products. Eventually he became very wealthy but in so doing he never forgot his roots were in Hallamshire.

Thomas was baptised on September 4th 1634 at Rotherham where his parents, Thomas (a whitesmith) and Ellen, his wife, lived they having married on June 28th 1632. Ellen, baptised in 1588 was the sister of John Romsker, being two years younger. Both were among the children of John Romsker who, as already mentioned, married Isobel, a daughter of Rauf Greaves, of Hallfield, in 1585. John and Isobel were both born in the 1560s. So, there you have as promised, the third of our bonus stories and with it a direct link between Hallfield and Harvard University, Mass.

AND FINALLY........

Before embarking on this project I predetermined that the mid-19th century should be the date I would 'cover' up to and, thereafter, should opportunity present itself I would carry on with another, slim volume bringing readers as up to date as was possible. As it happened, however, I have obtained and included information about many of the properties we have 'visited' post that date with one exception, that of Hallfield. Here, much research still needs to be done but I can reveal that a known occupier following the Woodhead family was one Robert Newman, described as Agent to Earl Fitzwilliam. That was certainly between 1833 and 1841. Whether he continued to live there I cannot say but between 1849 and 1862 his address is not shown, simply his trade, being that of a woodman.

Street Directories inform us that in 1849 in Bradfield Dale fourteen men were listed as being farmers with one besom maker and three quarry owners. The number of farmers (of both sexes) had increased to 18 in 1862 and also living in the Dale was the besom maker and the constable. So quite a lot of people who owned, rented, worked the dale land were to be affected by the construction of Dale Dike Reservoir.

I was tempted to take a 'peep' and see, in 1896, who the occupants were of some of the properties we have 'looked' at and the Directory for that year is quite informative. Thornseat has listed a couple of farmers, George Birley and George Horsfield. At Smallfield the two farmers were Henry Elliott and Benjamin Bramhall. Bradfield Dale was the home of a family long established in Bradfield, the Bacons, and here resided George Bacon. Mark Booth, too, was in the vicinity. Down at Oaks was farmer, Mrs J. Elliott while Ugghill Hall was occupied by a very busy chap, George Elliott who, it appears, was a carrier, a farmer and a grocer! Mrs Jane Horsfield was not only the victualler at the Strines Inn but also, following the tradition of that place, a farmer. Two more farmers I have spotted living/working in Bradfield Dale were Reuben Booth and Benjamin Waterhouse. There is no mention of Hallfield but at our other oft-mentioned farm-residence, Woodseats, lived Henry Creswick and Jonathan Crawshaw.

Mrs Robinson, of Woodseats Farm tells me that much land belonging to Brogging was 'swallowed up' by Dale Dike Reservoir and that the house became a dam keeper's lodge.

During the course of our journey I have said getting more details about this place or that was being undertaken. Unfortunately, no responses were ever received.

One addition and that to the couple of paragraphs under the heading of 'HALLEFELDE – early mentions of'. The Bradfield Local History Group's publication is called 'Bygones of Bradfield'.

If I may make a recommendation it is that, having now read through this little booklet you afford yourself an opportunity to take an unhurried look at the original, hand written 98pp manuscript upon which it is based. There you could find more, or varied information about the places visited and the people we have met. Additionally helpful too there is an extensive index covering some 690 alphabetical entries.

ACKNOWLEDGEMENTS

UPON reflection I find it really is an impossibility to enumerate those very kind individuals who, over the past sixty years have helped me so much with the collecting (and subsequent documenting) of the local history especially of the three localities mentioned in the Preface. Therefore, I think the best solution is to offer my most grateful thanks and appreciation to the following:

All the residents of Wadsley Village who so freely talked about themselves and their families, many of whom had lived thereabouts generation following generation for over 150 years. We discussed a huge range of subjects ranging from local industry to church/chapel going, characters to poverty, schooling to entertainment. Many I called upon during the late-1960s before they left the district and the cottage-homes they had lived in all their lives only to move to areas unknown. All this being brought about by the Compulsory Purchase Orders which were issued in that decade, the local authority considering that many of the properties were unfit for occupation and, therefore, had to be demolished. That story, the rebuilding of Wadsley Village I penned for inclusion in the booklet: A Wisewood Diary, published by Wisewood School.

Newspapers and magazines have played no small part in publishing items deemed to be of interest and so, naturally, I thank most cordially the editors from time to time of the Morning

Telegraph, Sheffield Telegraph, The Star, Sheffield Spectator, South Yorkshire Times (Penistone, Stocksbridge and Hoyland edition), Wadsley Parish News and many others beyond South Yorkshire.

Local radio too, has been invaluable in communicating with the local populace and I am indebted, here, to many a producer and presenter of various regular programmes transmitted by BBC Radio Sheffield.

And, just what would we do without our libraries and archive services, many of whom Nationwide have been most helpful? A special thank you, though to the libraries at Eckington, Rotherham and Matlock (Local Studies) and it goes without saying to our own, Sheffield Local Studies, the Arts, Social Sciences and Sports Library and Archives section at Shoreham Street. Whenever I've popped into either of them, always the same friendly and most helpful service.

Generous, too, with helpful responses to so many questions put to him has been the Archivist to Bradfield Parish Council, Malcolm Nunn. I am indebted to him.

OTHER LOCAL HISTORY BOOKS BY THE AUTHOR

Apart from titles already mentioned in the book the following may be of interest:

CABBAGE HILL (1976) The story of the folk who lived at Studfield Hill, characters, local industry, the village fair and why Cabbage Hill.

CANDLES, CORVES AND CLOGS (1981) This was produced by members of the Wisewood Methodist Church from a manuscript given to them upon the subject of ganister mining in the area and a history of the Wadsley Park Ganister Mine.

WADSLEY CHURCH IN VICTORIAN TIMES (1984) Written to mark the 150th Anniversary of the opening of Wadsley Parish Church.

AND A FINAL 'THANK YOU'

I wish to express my grateful appreciation to those persons who have shown interest in and donated most kindly practical assistance, with the story you have read:

Mrs Margaret Peter for creating, with infinite patience, the fine line drawings based on the Shield of Arms of the Worrall family and which is inscribed above the porch of the Strines Inn, and from the photographs of Hallfield House, St Nicholas Church and the Watch House and of Woodseats Farm taken and/or supplied by Mr & Mrs Andrew Duckenfield, Mrs Isobel Pentreath and by Mrs Gillian Robinson, respectively.

Bob Horton, who made a special visit to Bradfield Dale to photograph the beautiful and contrasting scenery of the region. From the resultant and delightful set of images have been selected those views which adorn the cover of our booklet.

My thanks too to Mrs Jo Burns for typing the manuscript, to Rebecca Kay and Stephanie White for much preparatory work, and to Keith Stubley of Northend for guiding the book through to final copies.

The net proceeds from the sale of the booklet are to be given to Heart and Leukaemia Charities to further help with their excellent research into treatments.

ADDENDUM:

The interpretation of heraldic insignia and symbols is both complex and time consuming and in the instance of the Worrall Family we have no idea when the Coat of Arms was granted, presumably by the English College of Arms. The composition however, is set forth as being: 'A lion rampant between three cups, impaling on a chevron, three trefoils; in chief an arm in armour, embowed between two wings, holding a dagger bendwise within a bordure engrailed, crest on helmet with mantling a cup.' All of which must tell us something about those members of the Worrall family who lived hundreds of years ago. I shall 'bow out' by asking each reader to arrive at their own conclusion based on the meanings of some of the symbols mentioned as comprising the design on the shield (main part of the achievement): Lion (deathless courage), Rampant (rearing) Cups (Holy Communion/Mass) Chevron (a bent stripe), Trefoil (three leaflets/clover) Chief (upper one third of shield) Arm in armour (wearing gauntlet and ready for military action), Wings (celebrity, sometimes protection), Bordure (edge of different colour round the shield), Crest (ornamental device above helmet) Mantling (scrollwork). Shield also signifies a defender. Having sorted that one out try the arms originally awarded to nameholders and that comprised... blazon of a gold field, charged with two lions passant guardant in black, on a blue chief, three covered cups, gold'. Whether it was used by the Worralls of the Sheffield area or the Worralls of the Wirral peninsula is debatable.

I wish you well with your quest and I would like to hear what you make of it all.